Young Children and Spirituality

Young Children and Spirituality

Barbara Kimes Myers

ROUTLEDGE
New York and London

Published in 1997 by

Routledge
29 West 35th Street
New York, NY 10001

Published in Great Britain in 1997 by

Routledge
11 New Fetter Lane
London EC4P 4EE

Printed in the United States of America
Design: Jack Donner

Library of Congress Cataloging-in-Publication Data
is available from the Library of Congress

For Joyce Cain,
whose wisdom and caring presence
go with her students and colleagues.
We miss the sound of her laughter.

Contents

Preface

I have written this book for those in the secular world who are concerned about the ability of young children to thrive. These people include parents and other family members, school and social-service employees, early-childhood researchers, teacher educators, medical personnel, corporate planners, and employees of government agencies. It will also be useful as a community resource and in college courses and seminars in child development, family studies, and early-childhood education.

This is a book for anyone who seeks a theoretical and practical language to talk about spiritual development in the early years of life. It is for those who grew up within religious traditions but who do not find the language of their tradition useful in their relationships with young children. It is also for those who have grown up in a traditional religious institution, who do value their religious language, and who want to communicate with others outside their tradition about the human spirit, spirituality, and spiritual development.

This volume began to take shape almost three decades ago through my conversations with Dr. Margaret B. McFarland at the Arsenal, a child-study center at the University of Pittsburgh. Dr. McFarland was a professor and mentor to many people who worked with young children, including myself. She brought a deep understanding of the dynamics of child development to her relationships with all of us. She also shared a long history of complex experiences with young children and families, a sense of wonder, the ability to communicate, and a deep respect for the personhood of the young child.

During my early professional life as a teacher I recognized that young children brought all of their being—including the spiritual—into the so-called secular settings of which I was a part, including Operation Head Start programs, the primary classroom, and hospitals. However, in our society any explicit talk about the spiritual development of young children was relegated to religious institutions or deemed inappropriate for discussion within the secular world.

As a Judeo-Christian layperson who has been involved with a number of local churches over the past thirty years, I have known many parishioners who have worked with young children in secular settings. Whether teachers and administrators in the public schools, medical doctors and nurses, people in the field of law, developers of public policy, or business personnel, they all seemed to deliberately avoid sharing their concerns about the spiritual development of young children. Spirituality was something that had to remain inside the realm of religious institutions though many of us sensed the importance of the spiritual in the secular worlds of our work.

A number of books about young children and spirituality, including one I coauthored with my theologian husband, have been published by religious presses. These books are for people who work within religious institutions. They employ religious language that is often either unfamiliar to readers outside organized religion or that has been rejected by those who no longer feel it is relevant to their lives.

I also know many people in the secular world who sense that there is a spiritual dimension of child development in addition to the physical, social, emotional, and cognitive aspects. Although they are working to put their thoughts about spirituality and the young child into words, they are struggling to do so.

Until there are ways to understand and name spiritual life within the secular world, a dynamic component of development will remain ignored. This severely limits our ability to address issues related to the "whole child"—even as we claim that this is what we do. Such an important aspect of human development deserves to be explored both in theory and practice. Once this occurs, our understanding of child development and the resulting professional and practical conversations will be more complete.

This book provides a framework for the discussion of spirit and spirituality in the lives of our youngest children. At its heart lies a theoretical perspective that delineates spiritual development as an integral component of every child's life. The conversation that began in Dr. McFarland's office continue in this volume. Over the years, I have lived and worked with young children, taught and learned from the adults in their lives, and struggled with policymakers to find new ways to serve the youngest members of our society and their families.

The development of such a framework and the accompanying language is ongoing. As I work with my own undergraduate and graduate students at DePaul University and talk with people in many different child and family-focused settings, I continue to learn from the process. My hope is that what you find in these pages will be useful in your work as well.

Many young children and families are present in this book, and I thank them for their stories. Colleagues and friends merit considerable thanks for their input as well. These include Karen Maurer, Mary Pat Martin, Sr Frances Ryan, Margit Kir-Stimon, Gayle Mindes, Theodore Jennings, and Dow Edgerton.

Others also contributed to this work in a variety of ways. The faculty and administration of DePaul University provided a leave from my university responsibilities which allowed me to concentrate on writing. George Brown and his colleagues at Western Theological Seminary in Holland, Michigan, gifted me with a quiet office and the use of their research library. My deep appreciation goes to Philip Rappaport, who initially saw possibilities for this book, and to Christine Cipriani and others at Routledge who saw it through to publication.

You will meet my family here, especially Michal Elaine, Melissanne and Jason William Myers, and I thank them for learning with me. As always, William R. Myers has contributed significantly to my work through his support, knowledge, critique, insight, and presence.

one

Invitations

Spring seems far off, impossible, but it is coming. Already there is dusk instead of darkness at five in the afternoon; already hope is stirring at the edges of day.

—Kathleen Norris

I remember thinking when I was very young—maybe five or six—that I could not wait until I grew up because then I would know everything. Adults seemed to be all-knowing, a perspective that provided considerable security. And then I grew up and found out that adults do not have all of the answers; rather, what adults come to know is how to live and work with a hopefulness that stirs on the edges of experience.

As a young woman, I went to college to learn how to teach young children. Several years later, having been immersed in working with kindergarten and primary age children and their parents in the public schools of western Pennsylvania and New York, I looked at my classroom of second-graders. I thought about Randall, who seemed so tired all of the time; Eddie, with his eagerness to learn to read and deep distress when he could not; Mary, whose penetrating questions demanded honesty; Louise, who pulled away from human touch to an inner world that would not let me or any of her classmates in; Demonde, who was highly inventive in studying the bird's nest outside of our window even as he had difficulty focusing on our class activities. If I were to teach so that these children could thrive, I needed to understand them better. So I studied how children develop and spent much more time with young children, their parents, their teachers, their pediatricians, and others involved in that development.

Today, I know that just when I think I understand two-year-olds, three-year-olds, or young children of any age, I meet a little person whose actions will prompt a sense of wonder, puzzlement, or perplexity in me about what might be going on in this unique mind. Such an experience pushes me to the edge of what I know and challenges me to move beyond what I have learned about the physical, cognitive, and socio-emotional development of young children. Personal experience, knowledge of theory, and the world of professional practice provide words, symbols, and conceptualizations for my thought at such times, but they are not enough to catch the essence of such moments. As I reflect on such occasions, perhaps my own three children, now young adults, have been my greatest teachers.

The Flood

The washing machine in our third-floor apartment on Bayview Avenue emptied into the kitchen sink. On several occasions it had overflowed, creating a floor full of water to be mopped, as well as legitimate outrage from our usually congenial neighbors below. During one of these overwhelming moments when the water poured over the sink and flooded the kitchen, our two-year-old daughter helped me see beyond the moment.

I remember her confident statement, "You be all right mommy," and the incisive eyes and small hand that touched me as I exhaustedly leaned beyond my pregnant body to rescue a bag of green beans. There was an assuredness, a strength, a spiritedness in this small child that was not accounted for in child development theory.

This is not to suggest that my daughter was some sort of mystical child who had been chosen by an undefinable cosmic being in order to make some special "truth" available only to an elect few. Such a sense of assuredness, strength, and spiritedness can be discerned in children everywhere when it is not squelched, nullified, neglected, or in other ways repudiated or overlooked. When I share my flooded-kitchen story with other professionals in fields that are informed by the study of child development; they, too, often remember an event with a child in their own lives with characteristics similar to my two-year-old daughter's.

This was the case with Marty's teacher. In a recent conversation she described three-year-old Marty as having arrived in her classroom in early September much like a small, compact whirlwind of energy. It was as if the classroom was a smorgasbord of delicious activities for him, and Marty's plate was never quite full enough. He was always reaching for more . . . more clay, more blocks, more cups at the water table, more "trike" time.

One time as his mother picked him up at the day's end, his teacher noticed him eyeing a water fountain. She asked, "Marty, would you like a drink of water?"

"Yes," he responded, moving toward the fountain, "a drink."

The teacher pulled a small step stool to the fountain so that he could climb up and get a drink. When he was finished drinking and splashing a bit in the water, he climbed backward down the few steps to the floor. As the teacher reached for the stool to put it away, Marty stopped her and said, "Leave it here . . . 'body else might want a drink, too."

On the Edges of Knowing

And so the actions of these two young children (my daughter and Marty) challenge the conceptualization of egocentrism that Anna Freud, Jean Piaget, and others have described as being characteristic of young children. While adults who knew them could confirm that egocentrism certainly was present on many occasions in the thinking of these two young children, the point is that such a descriptive theoretical construct is incomplete. There is something else resting on the edges of our theoretical frameworks which must be considered.

Perhaps that is because when child development theorists describe what it means to be human, they are struggling to offer interpretive, but necessarily incomplete, structures. No one theory does it all. Such structures are helpful, for they give us ways to think and talk about young children and their families in our personal and professional lives. But while these conceptualizations can be suggestive, they cannot replace the particularity that is the life of an actual child. There is always more available in one specific life than can be understood at any given time.

Many of the understandings that we presently hold about young children come through the rich descriptions provided by people including Anna Freud, Maria Montessori, Erik Erikson, Jean Piaget, and others. These giants of child development paid careful attention to young children and conscientiously documented their observations. Today, other theory-builders such as Peggy Miller and Howard

Gardner join in this on-going process. And, as we read their work, we discover a sense of awe in their recorded descriptions as well as a respect for the personhood of those young children who initially informed their theoretical frameworks. Yet, when theories are woodenly applied by those who try to emulate the initial theory-builders, the richness of a particular child's play and the uniqueness of how that child engages in the activities of early childhood can often be lost.

This occurs when theories and research findings are dogmatically applied and, as a result, lose the spiritedness, wonder, aliveness, and relevance that gave birth to them in the first place. This often happens because we inadvertently allow theories to become blinders rather than lenses. Our use of theory may result in missing the "something new" that could be bubbling on the edge of the subject (not the object) of all such effort; that is, we often miss the child.

Danger: Theories As Locked Boxes

An extremely competent mother of three daughters and the holder of a Master of Social Work degree, Ann Ito, tells her own story, one that poignantly illustrates the danger involved when a person in authority rigidly applies theory. Ann, blind since shortly after her birth, was delighted when her three-year-old daughter spontaneously—through the child's interactions with her mother at breakfast—began to read the labels on the breakfast cereal boxes. When Ann enthusiastically relayed this information to the child's teacher, the teacher admonished the mother for inappropriately pushing her child. In the teacher's words, "Reading is not an appropriate activity for three-year-olds." There was no room for Ann's unique experience with her daughter because it did not fit, and in fact clashed, with this teacher's interpretation of child development theory.

Theories as Edges

If we must have pat answers (that is, if everything has to "fit" a particular theoretical construct) we can miss the surprises and challenges that lie beyond the edges of our knowledge. But when we are well informed by theory and research in child development and are also open to the aliveness of young children and their relationship with their families, then it is reasonable to expect that we can helpfully engage in co-creating a definition of what it means to be human beings who are in ever-expanding and growing relationships with young children.

Such exploration on the margins of what we know allows those who live and work with young children to accept the position of becoming informal researchers even as they explore this edge; that is, they might be investigating what we still don't know even as they ask questions related to the children in their care. Such questioning (when clearly identified and reflected upon) often has the potential to move us beyond the current knowledge base of child development and early-childhood education inherited from those who came before. Such explorative reflection also helps one make better decisions about the practices that are appropriate for young children in any given time and place. Such practices are enhanced when we are open to the diversity of the children's backgrounds. Occasionally, however, the practices of cultures other than our own present us with situations that seem to go against our understandings of what is good for young children.

Missing the Edge: On Understanding Beans

In the program that Bertha Gapara, an early-childhood professional in Zimbabwe directs, young children name, count, plant, and play in various ways with what seems to be an infinite number of beans. During a visit to Zimbabwe,

I watched this scene and recognized that such activities would be viewed as inappropriate in the U.S.A. In my country, child care workers would worry that the children might put a bean in an ear or nostril. Yet, young children in this center have never, in the twenty years of its existence, done such a thing.

While beans were inexpensive, a regular part of daily existence, and a ready resource for the classroom, the director nevertheless recounted a situation when a well-known early-childhood authority from the U.S.A. visited the center and became quite critical of the staff for permitting the children to use beans. "Beans" according to the expert, "were unsafe." Dr. Gapara considered the woman's remarks and then chose to ignore them, for in her words, "children played with beans at home, knew the names of beans, knew how their mothers used them, and used beans sensibly."

When child development theory and research lead us to make proclamations such as: "This is the stage when all children should begin reading," "These are appropriate activities for all children in all places," and "Beans are unsafe for children in every culture," then we miss the particularity (the edge) of what is going on in that specific situation.

Erikson's Challenge: To Be on the Edge of Our Own Understanding

Erik Erikson was a psychoanalyst who built his bio-psychosocial theory of human development on the work of Freud. He can be helpful as we consider the dynamics of what children bring with them when they meet us at the edge of our understanding. Erikson (1964) suggests that we and our children meet at our own particular age or stage of development even as we interactively move each other along. He terms this interactive process "cogwheeling."

By this term Erikson suggests an image of two (or more)

intermeshed wheels, the cogs of which are in the closest of proximity, and without which proximity neither cog would turn. Erikson's image of "cogwheeling" helps us understand that our relationships with children are interactive and that children are not the only ones engaged in the developmental process. Yet the cogwheeling image is flat, one-dimensional, and overly controlled when applied to the messiness of human experience. Erikson must have thought so, too, since in his later writing (1985), he used the term "developmental dialogue" as a more multi-layered description of the relational "cogwheeling" process. His sense of "developmental dialogue" suggests the aliveness of the "cogwheeling" relationship even as it extends the image from the mechanical to the personal, leaving room for the depth and dimension of human experiences.

Erikson has often come under fire, perhaps unjustifiably so, since like the rest of us (as he so clearly taught), he worked within a specific social context. But, if we look closely at Erikson's writing, we find that while he has a clear and tight theory and was articulate in sharing, he was always pushing himself, his critics, and his readers to lean out into the uncharted space beyond that theory. Could there be other ideas about how and why something might be happening? It is as if he asks us to imagine "what if?" After Erikson died, this question led his wife, Joan Erikson, a long-time partner in living and learning (as well as editor of his writing), to suggest a ninth stage—a stage or age in the human life cycle that focuses on what it is like to be on the edge of dying.

Erikson's work encourages us to recognize that when we engage in relationships with young children (or children of any age) the child within us—that child of a similar age— also has a developing edge that enters into our newly emerging relationship with these young people. This awareness gifts us with the ability to empathize with children, to play with them, and to consider options for guiding and teaching them. It also challenges us to think about what we are like and what we want our children to be like.

Within the child, deep inside of us, there are irrational fears to be examined, confusing messages to be understood, as well as feelings of joy, anxiety, and puzzlement that we cannot name. As adults—parents, teachers, care givers, or providers of resources for the next generation—we transcend our present reality even as we cogwheel on the very edge of our being. And, as we engage in this relational process, we help our youngest children transcend those particular realities that block or hinder their growth. These developmental dialogues are to be treasured, even though they are the rich underpinnings of the most common moments in our everyday lives. For example, while thousands of children may take their first steps on any given day, when a child we know takes her first step, that day has special significance. That step is more than just a step.

First Steps Need Helping Hands

Reaching upward from the floor where she has been crawling, ten-month-old Christina winds her pudgy fingers around the edge of the sofa. Gripping the sofa firmly she pulls her body upright. Her legs tremble, but she holds on until she is steady. Supporting herself, she carefully places one hand as far as she can reach; then—sliding the other, hand over hand—Christina cruises around the cushioned seat and stops at the end. She sucks on her lower lip, pauses and fixes her gaze on her grandfather who is seated in a chair just beyond the sofa's edge.

With one hand gripping the furthest reaches of the supporting cushion, she reaches toward her grandfather with the other until, for a moment, she lets go of the sofa and stands alone. Tumbling down, Christina giggles with delight. Responding to her grandfather's encouraging smile and playful laugh as he leans toward her, she places both hands in his and pulls herself upward as he gently lifts her back into an upright position.

All of us, like Christina, initially move away from and then back to our loved ones by crawling, "inch-worming," or scooting on our bottoms, but eventually we figure out how to stand on our own feet. We also tumble down in our initial efforts to walk. Nevertheless, when Christina falls to the floor, she intuitively responds to the positive invitation of a world represented by her grandfather that invites her to explore not only the environment in which she finds herself but her own capacities as well.

But grandfather also grows through this relationship. Christina's grandfather thrives in his confidence as a grandfather—as a person who senses his own integrity, and who cares for and supports the learning of the next generation. With this internal integration of the experience into his own identity comes renewed hope for a future that extends beyond his own life time. This happens even as Christina develops confidence in herself and in her world. Together, through such "cogwheeling," they participate in a relational developmental dialogue of their own creation, not in any lock step way, but fluently from the depth of lived experience within the social context and historical space of their time. This occurs as granddaughter and grandfather explore what the newness of this relationship means for them.

It will not be long before Christina will be taking her first steps. Then all of the world with its vast array of nooks and crannies will continue to invite her exploration. No longer will cruising around the sofa's edge be enough. She and those who love her and continue to help her will engage in the on-going process of transcendence.

Transcendence

The theologian Bernard Lonergan (1972) suggests that like Christina and her grandfather all human beings yearn for more. Lonergan builds his theological thinking upon what he calls our innate human dissatisfaction with ourselves and our world. For Lonergan the very process of living implies transcendence. The word transcendence derives from the Latin word "transcendere," which means, "to climb over." And young children do "climb over" and reach out into their world on an ongoing basis. The word transcendence, therefore, can be used by us to name a process of going over, beyond, or through various limits or obstacles. As we have seen in the developmental cogwheeling of Christina and her grandfather, relationships with caring others support us in the process.

But to be useful, such a process must be born out of appropriate adult-supported openness, rather than authoritarian control. Often, we as adults wonder at what is taking place within the child beyond the boundaries of our own bodies and thought. While interrelated with our children, we are not them and they are not us. But when we look carefully, and provide trustworthy environments, we can move beyond our own consciousness of an event (and what it ought to look like) and connect to what that experience might mean to the child. We can be more open to the "difference" of a child if, as we enter an experience with one, we encourage ourselves to sense and call into memory a warm remembrance of a presence that supported our own exploration. Developmental growth (the process of transcendence) occurs as adults relationally interact in hopeful ways with children, even as the children do things that occasionally challenge adult perspectives.

Embracing Wonder

Daniel's father watches in amazement as his eleven-month-old son systematically drops each one of the peas from his high chair tray on to the floor. Leaning forward, Daniel surveys each pea's descent and its landing before carefully grasping another between his finger and thumb and then releasing it. Instead of erupting in anger, however, this wise father senses that for Daniel something new is being learned at lunchtime about Daniel's own capabilities and about space. Daniel is also deeply engaged in transcendence. He (like his father and Christina and her grandfather) engages in this process in a "spirited" fashion.

The Process of Transcendence

Philip Phenix (1974) sees "spirit" as the word that names the "property of limitless going beyond" (p. 118). Phenix maintains that all of us, regardless of our age, are engaged in the process of transcendence. He holds that: "It is phenomenologically not the case that some persons, called 'religious' or 'spiritual' types, experience [transcendence] and others do not." Phenix argues that "human consciousness is rooted in transcendence, and that the analysis of all human consciousness discloses the reality of transcendence as a fundamental presupposition of the human condition" (p. 122).

When Christina and Daniel are said to have "spirit," for Phenix this means that they express "perennial discontent and dissatisfaction with any and every finite realization" (Phenix, 1974, p. 118). "Spirit" is what allows Christina to "giggle with delight" as she pulls herself upright once again. It also fuels Daniel's patient study of the velocity of falling peas.

As Jerome Berryman (1985) suggests, young children "live at the limit of their experiences most of the time" (p. 126). I would add that their parents, grandparents and other members of their caring communities do as well. As adults we have our own learning experiences of holding on and letting go—and perhaps just watching a bit. We anticipate some of the developmental dialogues that occur, but we are also surprised by experiences with young children that cannot be planned or expected.

So it is that our adult lives "cogwheel" with those young children in our care. Ours is the responsibility for providing physically, emotionally, and socially safe places for them to explore; for setting protective safeguards until they can maintain appropriate limits for themselves; and, for providing a language for naming the experiences, and a values system that informs their rudimentary choices. We do all of this within family networks that share our deep love for the chldren who are special to us, even as we hope for their future.

two

Hopeful Contexts

. . . Our mothers look out of our eyes when we love our children, and we discover how much they loved us in how we love our own.

—Frederick Turner

Hope is the assured sense that one can transcend the present situation. Hope is what helps us when we worry about the future. Hope keeps us going, but it is more than a simple belief in a future. Erikson tells us that such hope is "the ontogenetic basis of faith . . . nourished by the adult faith which pervades patterns of care" (1963, p. 118).

In their delightful book *So Much,* author Trish Cooke and illustrator Helen Oxenbury (1994) create a feeling for this unique nourishing of a child's spirit within the context of the family.

When we turn the first page of Cooke's book, Mom and baby aren't doing much at all. Then the door bell rings. There's someone at the door.

The clear, bright, uncomplicated words and pictures introduce us to an aunt who wants to squeeze the baby and who sits the baby on her knee and reads a story. We meet an uncle who wants to kiss the baby and we share baby's delight in this familiar person.

Granma and a great aunt arrive at the door and reach out to the gleeful baby. They want to eat the baby, and the baby dances with them. Cousins enter next and burst across the page in sneakers and baseball cap and want to " . . . fight the baby."

And the baby tussles with the cousins on the floor. We see the feet of the nearby adults in the background of the colorful illustration.

And so the house becomes full of familiar folk. Then the door bell rings again. Mom picks up the baby and everybody waits as she opens the door.

A turn of the page and we find everyone gathered around Daddy, who has a briefcase in hand. Baby, in Mom's arms, reaches for his coat lapel. The next page has Daddy on the floor . . . his striped socks showing as he stretches and folds his legs to engulf barefooted baby in his lap. Mom can be seen carrying a birthday cake and other goodies in the back ground.

We see joyful figures celebrating on the next page, and the words:

> And when it was time
> for them to go
> and everybody tired . . .
> the baby wanted to play
> some more.

But Mom carries an unhappy baby to bed where baby plays with a teddy bear and remembers everybody saying they wanted to "SQUEEZE and KISS and EAT and FIGHT him. . . ."

We turn the page to read, "because they loved him SO MUCH!" The final picture has baby asleep—with teddy— while Daddy leans on the crib and Mom tucks in the sheet.

Walter Bruggemann (1985) suggests that as members of families, caring adults "practice a peculiar vocation," the creation of a "communal network of memory and hope in which individual members may locate themselves and discern their identities" (p. 8). It is within such contexts that the spirit of our youngest children is nurtured and occasions of transcendence take place.

The occasions of transcendence discussed so far may sound euphorically optimistic, but they also occur in negative circumstances. Nevertheless, transcendence suggests that even the most negative occasion need not remain toxic and continually painful. Negative experiences often result in a deepening crisis of the spirit which has the ability to provide sufficient energy to search for positive contexts within which the ongoing process of transcendence can be engaged. This is where young children come to identify with hope and not with despair. Thus identity has a location, the cultural context mediated by family, surrounding the child.

The family bring its values into its shaping of the world; no social context is ever value free. Every "communal network of memory and hope," while part of the larger culture, has a story all its own.

In *So Much*, Trish Cooke's story and Helen Oxenbury's illustrations tell us that love is present when people care for each other and that the embodiment of such love is a primary function of the family. Through a simple story we see that meaning can be discovered in the ways the members of an extended family care for one another. Storytelling is one way caring adults begin to share the meaning of being human with young children. Story is also one way we can talk about spirituality.

The stories we honor and prize call our children into being. Story re-orders, sifts through experience, and allows others, young children and adults alike, to hear what we think truly matters. We are constituted by the stories we tell ourselves and others. Thus stories serve an ontological purpose. Story connects us with that which lies beyond ourselves and this process makes us ask questions about the meanings of our lives. It is, in fact, a way we can begin to define what we mean when we use the term "spirituality."

In its broadest definition, spirituality is "a code word for the depth dimension of human existence" (Becker, 1994, p. 257). The adjectives humans use to more clearly define spirituality (Jesuit spirituality, men's spirituality, Buddhist spirituality) are attempts to locate access points and disciplined approaches to this depth dimension. After such labeling, spirituality remains an inexhaustible, socially constructed web of meaning that holds rich relational resources for us whenever one plumbs it to its depth. This relational web supports us and our children as we spiritedly move into and through occasions of transcendence. But our engagement in transcendence is fatally flawed without the presence of empathy and imagination.

As we shall see later, various spiritualities emphasize different aspects of this web of relationships. At this point it is enough to note that numerous languages exist to describe spirituality and the process of transcendence and that it is within human experience that human spirit flourishes.

What Matters

Helen Goggin is a Canadian theologian and educator who builds on the work of Marjorie Suchocki (1994). Goggin suggests that "memory, empathy and imagination are the aspects of human consciousness that enable us to live in harmony and cooperation with one another" (1994, p. 4). Thus it is not enough for those of us who, in Bruggemann's words, "practice a peculiar vocation," to create a "communal network of memory and hope." It is also necessary to empathize with our infants, toddlers, and other young children in ways that allow them to know that we understand their ways of communicating.

This means that in our interactions with young children we respect their feelings of the moment, and when they are able, we help them to name these feelings. We also guide them as they learn to act on their feelings in productive ways. This is not a one-step process. It involves being with young children in ongoing ways in order to understand the ways in which they are communicating with us.

With the very young infant, we must pick up on subtle cues and respond to cries and gurgles. A two-year-old needs us to listen and respond to newly learned words and to model language and social skills. Preschoolers need physical and emotional safety to try out their own experience through play.

Empathizing with our youngest children involves imagining what their experiences are like and what kind of meaning they are assigning to the environments we provide. It is imagination that moves us and our young children beyond memory, through empathy, toward the transcendence of the present moment.

This is why play is so important for young children. When they can maintain mental images (at about two-and-a-half), they can then play with those mental images in the concrete world of experience (much like Cooke's and Oxenbury's baby who remembers the family members wanting to "SQUEEZE and KISS and EAT and FIGHT" him). In a negative context, such words could instill fear. In the context of *So Much*, these words help construe a social location of hope and care. Meaning evolves from such location. Thus memory, empathy and imagination are as Goggin suggests, "interdependent factors in our experience of the world" (p. 4). It is through play that young children become adept at imagining. It is through imagination that we, as adults, can consider new possibilities and transcend our present reality.

Kieran Egan (1992) gives us a definition of imagination that helps us understand its importance in any learning situation—that process of moving from the known to the unknown:

> . . . imagination is the capacity to think of things as possibly being so; it is an intentional act of mind; it is the source of invention, novelty, and generativity; it is implicated in all perception and in the construction of meaning; it is not distinct from rationality but rather a capacity that greatly enriches rational thinking. (p. 3)

Participatory Knowing

Children develop as whole human beings in relation to people who love, listen, respond to, and guide them. Such relationships require young children to engage their world, making meaning through interaction with that which is "other." In this process, young children experience not only concrete people and things, but smells, tastes, and tactile feelings, and images. In addition, there are verbal and non-verbal communications with those who are members of their ongoing web of relationships. The "other" also

includes internal feelings and ways of understanding that
have not yet developed or been explored.

As Piaget carefully documented and others have confirmed, young children take the world in through their
senses and experience their own bodies in relation to what
they see, touch, taste, hear, and smell. They are developing
through what Douglas Sloan (1989) terms "participatory
knowing" (p. 7). It is their lived experiences with their own
bodies, other people, and all of life's invitations for transcendence, through which they come to make sense of their
worlds. While that sense (arrived at as a young child) may
not always be easily accessible as they grow older, it flavors
all of their future knowing. These experiences are founda-
tional for all learning. Gradually, with our help, young children sort out and learn to name feelings, behaviors, people,
and things they have encountered and engendered in the
process.

We can understand much of what young children are experiencing through our observation of their behavior. This
is especially so when we make connections to the knowledge base of child development that has evolved over the
years. Yet, no matter how well we know this theory and research, we do not have access to the workings of the minds
of young children.

Think with me about young children as they examine the
physical properties of mud puddles. They step and stomp
and splash in mucky water, dragging sticks through the
damp sludge and tossing pebbles with anticipation of the
coming plop as the small stones sink out of sight. We can
only imagine what sense they are making of the experience.

We understand that knowledge about the mud puddles
and sinking stones is what we have come to call physical
knowledge. What one's friends, and brothers and sisters
and others do together and the way they interact in the

process of engaging in mud puddle play is what we have come to call social knowledge. But how one feels about the mud puddle experience is personal knowledge. It is within the realm of personal knowledge that all other areas of knowledge become integrated, and it is within this realm that we can further examine "spirit" and the related term "spirituality."

Personal Knowledge

Philip Phenix (1964) contrasts personal meaning with impersonal meaning: "Personal knowledge is always on a one-to-one basis. It is not predicated upon the idea of 'anyone' or 'whosoever,' but on confrontation with the single being." He suggests that impersonal meanings "presuppose the interchangeability of persons" (p. 195). Thus, impersonal meanings can be understood as shared public understandings.

When we consider personal meaning in contrast to impersonal meaning we understand that each person who enters any relationship, either with others or with things, holds a unique understanding of that emerging relationship. The meaning of that knowing is inexhaustible. Never has there been anyone quite like this person or a conceptualization of the world quite like this person's. Never has there been quite an understanding of "self" or "self in relationship" as that held by such a unique individual. An infant, toddler or other young child is not simply formed by the experiences of life.

Our youngest children are co-creators of the experiences we share with them, for they bring their unique physical and personality characteristics as well as the strengths and challenges of their various intelligences. Through the engagement that Erikson has termed cogwheeling or developmental dialogue, people (adults and children) and things become other body subjects, rather than just objects of perception. Buber (1958) refers to this as an "I-thou relationship" in contrast with an "I-it" relationship in which the other has no "subjectiveness" and exists only as an object.

As a memory reminds me, even earthworms can be "thous," as they were for my young daughter some years ago. The "thouness" of self is also part of any encounter with memories even as it was part of my daughter's experience with something adults might view as mundane.

The "Thouness" of Earthworms and of Self

I remember our older daughter's first engagement with earthworms in her grandmother's garden when she was not yet two. She came across the wiggling worms after an evening shower; she felt invited to pick them up; they squirmed; she loosened her grasp and looked more closely; they began to crawl down her arm; she stooped down and gently placed them on the sidewalk, taking an even closer look, and the worms pulled and pushed themselves toward the nearby earth and slid out of sight.

Earthworms were the subject of her perception and there was a dialogue between the child and the worms. But her own feelings were also the subjects of her perception about her experience with earthworms and about being in her grandmother's garden with those of us who were also engaged in dialogue with her, each other, the world and with our own growing edges. With our help she gradually named her feelings and learned how to share them with others in life-enhancing ways. Today she is a teacher of young children who dig in gardens and explore earthworms; but more than this, she is a person who helps young children grow in hopeful ways.

three

Beyond "Momma Birding"

*... spirituality begins with our cultivating the inner
eye that sees everything as capable of being. ...*

—*Maria Harris*

My early years in higher education as a community college
professor in the Chicago area were marked with considerable exuberance as I conveyed my deep appreciation of
child development literature and practice to my students.
Despite my enthusiasm, it quickly became apparent that my
students did not always assign the same meaning to my
child development lectures that I had intended. With this
recognition came another—my students had a lot to teach
me. Even as I told them that there were multi-perspectives
on events as well as different ways of seeing, they were
teaching me from their own locations (multi-aged, multi-
cultural, multi-religious, multi-resourced, and multi-abled).
I was learning that the act of teaching is multi-vocal, and
that "to teach" is much more complex than the act of data

transfer. With this recognition came a growing awareness that my students were teaching me and each other more about social location than I alone was able to convey in my teaching about such multi-perspectives.

As I reflect on that experience today, perhaps what should have bothered me was that some of my initial students did take what I was saying as gospel. It was somehow as if what I taught them in those well-crafted lectures was "Truth" and that there were no other "truths."

Pre-Chewing, Pre-Digesting, and Stuffing

In the community college I was teaching child development in what I have come to call a "momma bird" fashion. The "momma bird" professes the canon of the field, including any of the difficult concepts that are to be metaphorically chewed up, predigested, and stuffed into the mouths of the waiting baby birds; i.e., the students. The lower the level of the student in the hierarchy of the college and university system, the greater the amount of chewing up, predigesting, and stuffing necessary.

While sharing knowledge of a professional field—such as child development—with people who will be expected to apply that knowledge in a variety of ways can be helpful, there are basic flaws in any extensive use of such an approach. The first flaw has to do with the question "Who holds the 'truth'?" or in other words, "Whose truth are we talking about?"

Variation on "Truth"

In the early 1970s I had not yet read Lev Vygotsky (1978) and Vasily Davydov (1995), but in a precursory and concrete way I understood the cultural and historical theory out of which he worked. I knew well that the place and time in history in which human personality develops cannot be avoided and that it impacts what we, as teachers and people who care for children, do in relation to them. Values and virtues emerge within such social contexts; so does the content and the form of the way a person thinks. Initially for me this knowledge came from growing up in two cultures.

By the time my younger brother and I had come along my family was firmly ensconced in the middle class of a small town in western Pennsylvania. But when we drove the winding road along the Allegheny River eighty miles further north to visit my mother's family, we entered a different world. The language basically was the same, but its use was more sparse and quite direct. The "shoulds" and "should nots" also differed.

At my grandparents' and aunts' and uncles' houses, my brother and I were free to run in the woods and along the winding dirt roads. Cousins Frankie Joe, Alice, Jeff, and my brother Jack and I played together, gathered eggs with my grandmother, picked fresh vegetables, and explored the beaver dams. At home in our small town of twenty thousand people there were social rules about what girls and boys could do or what to wear in particular settings. At my grandparents' there was a two-seated outhouse twenty feet from the front door and cold water continually ran from the spring through the single kitchen faucet. At home there was a bathroom shower, salmon colored toilet fixtures, and all of the hot water you could ever want.

Because my mother loved and valued her family, she taught my brother and me to behave appropriately in both the town and more rural areas. We learned to thrive in either setting. Through experiencing both places directly, my brother and I understood that there were alternative ways of doing things and different "truths." Neither was right or wrong, they were simply different.

Experiencing Other

Unfortunately, many undergraduate child development courses are still taught using the "momma bird" approach. This is especially true in large state universities where child development is "taught" in a large lecture hall to several hundred students.

Supporting this approach are at least a dozen child development texts, often written by university professors, and published by presses whose salesmen clamor to sell books and related materials to those within these institutions who are seduced by this top down approach. Textbooks are sought on the basis of how well they predigest the difficult and challenging controversies, the big words, conflicting ideas, and appropriate research findings. Accompanying teacher "guides" occasionally suggest interactive, small group exercises, but tests, usually purchased from the publisher, are electronically scored with answers being either right or wrong.

Textbooks and their accompanying materials can be helpful in presenting the formal knowledge from which professional practice is supposedly born. Yet, there is a great deal of personal knowledge about children, living, and working with young children that resides within the students themselves. They know about being little and vulnerable, being angry and confused, being lonely, being filled with joy, being anxious, being worried about behaviors that are "OK" and behaviors that are not "OK," and being concerned about non-verbal messages (such as gestures, facial expressions, and bodily stances).

Such knowledge implicitly and explicitly flavors—among other things—the ways in which we hold and carry infants, nurture the exploration of toddlers and respond to the intuitiveness of preschoolers. It also affects the ways we set limits; our perceptions of the roles of parents, grandparents, teachers, physicians, and other adults in the lives of young children; and, our understandings about what it means to be cared for and educated. Without these internal understandings about how we can negotiate the appropriate ways of doing particular things, we could easily be overwhelmed by life.

Reality: A Mental Construct?

George Kelly (1955) views people who are continually trying to make sense out of their worlds as scientists. For Kelly there is no objective, absolute reality but only reality as we construct it. Each person forms a mental construct of the world through their experiences and moves forward, trusting that the world has been constructed in a similar manner. Kelly stresses that such constructs are both cognitive and affective, implicit and explicit; and that human beings act out of the meaning that they individually assign the world. As a psychologist, Kelly concerns himself only with the way we construct reality. For him any "realness" in our contrived reality is finally unimportant. However, the philosopher, Merleau-Ponty (1962) argued that there is an absolute reality with which one can engage in a dialectic.

Engagement With Reality

For Merleau-Ponty, a person never fully knows that absolute reality. One can only gain further illumination of it. Making a phenomenon more explicit involves describing it from a variety of perspectives. For example, one might describe its history, its content, its configuration, its relationship to other phenomenon, or its likeness to or difference from other similar phenomena. Phenomenology (a term often used to categorize Merleau-Ponty's work) holds that reality involves an ongoing dialectic with that which is otherness. Through this dialectic other persons become other body subjects, rather than objects of perception. Merleau-Ponty would welcome Buber's description of the I-thou relationship described in Chapter One, primarily because Buber also thought in terms of reality as an ongoing dialectic with that which is otherness.

Both Kelly and Merleau-Ponty would agree that a person acts out of the meanings that she or he attributes to their world. Critically reflecting on the experiences of self and others in conjunction with the theories of Kelly and Merleau-Ponty allows us to move beyond what we know. Naming this process permits us to make our understandings public and to invite others to critically reflect on our ideas, insights and questions. Engaging in this critical dialectic keeps us honest, both with ourselves and with others. We also begin to question any uni-vocal approach to being with young children.

Getting Beyond Momma Birding

As a "momma birder" I cared about my students, but mine was a limited caring. Caring involves not only providing students with information from the knowledge base of child development, it also involves an engaged, critically reflective, developmental process complete with dispositions, understandings, and skills that will assist the one being cared for to care for both self and other. Even though what I presented to students as a young professor was well thought through and based on considerable scholarly work, in my initial teaching I had unfortunately not planned time, space, or a format for dialogue within which we all could learn.

My experience in dramatic acting in high school and speech training in college, along with a love of performance served me well as a "momma birder." This was especially true when I dramatically told stories that students connected to their own experiences. But in those "momma bird" years of teaching I was getting in the way of students touching the otherness of self and peers. I also duped myself out of the chance to learn from my students.

Perhaps rather than encouraging child development students to push toward the edges of our knowing as described in the preceding chapter, I was creating dogmatists like the teacher who scolded Ann Ito for prematurely teaching her daughter to read, or, the expert who chastised Dr. Gapara and her staff for using beans (see Chapter One). Another possibility is equally frightening.

Conceivably students might have left my child development class untouched by the richness and possibilities of the knowledge base of child development; i.e. the canon of the field. They might have come to view any formalized study of young children as irrelevant to their own construction of reality or only as the dominant culture's uni-vocal way of giving meaning to interactions with young children. Such an assumption could equate the theory and practice of the child development field with the tools of an oppressor.

If those studying child development are to enter into a spirituality of caring (see Chapter Five), then "momma bird" teaching is not enough. Learning takes place in a variety of ways as we explore self and other—even as the "other" includes those present and those who address us across the borders of times and places. By opening up the act of teaching, we explore the power of our own family and community myths in relation to our work with young children and their families. Through the sharing of experiences, the viewing of relevant videos, the reviewing of well developed case studies, the reading of original sources, and listening to guest discussants, we cogwheel with each other and the classroom becomes a community of scholars.

As a community of scholars we also benefit from exploring beyond the classroom and the university campus in a multitude of ways both together and individually. Through observing and reflecting on the lived worlds of young children, we can venture beyond and expand the constructed boundaries of our own worlds.

Intersubjective Spaces

Knowledge is co-created within what Lev Vygotsky (1978) describes as intersubjective space when together we establish a "zone of proximal development." Within such a zone, Vygotsky suggests that people who are moving from the known to the unknown are met in relation to what they can understand and do with help from a mentor, teacher, coach, or more knowledgeable peer. Such helping persons then provide what Jerome Bruner terms "scaffolding" so that learners can transcend their present understandings or skills.

In the process of providing such a "scaffolding," all involved bring something of value (dispositions, understandings, interests, skills, and dreams) to the relationship. And if we reflect on the process of transcendence as described in Chapter One, we might even think of Vygotsky's "zone of proximal development" as the space in which transcendence occurs.

Dwayne Heubner (1995) suggests, "The fact that we partake of the transcendent means that we are never complete, until death." He goes on to tell us, "We can always be more than we are." Considering the language of education, Huebner wants us to understand that, "'Learning' is a trivial way of speaking of the journey of the self.... We do not need 'learning theory' or 'developmental theory' to explain human change...." Huebner challenges us to take the language of education seriously when he advocates, "The question that educators need to ask is not how people learn and develop, but what gets in the way of the great journey—the journey of self or soul." Huebner further suggests that "education is a way of attending to and caring for the journey" (p. 18).

To the extent that "scaffolding" allows for such "attending to" and "caring for," the "scaffolding" image is useful. But when we reduce teaching to "momma birding," "attending and caring" are usually overlooked. University professors and other teachers are not the only ones who overuse "momma bird" techniques. Ways of dealing with young children and their families exist in a multitude of situations and settings. These include ways we "birth" babies, handle the separations of daily life, and the events surrounding death. They also include our ways of saying yes and no, the ways we affirm and limit behaviors, and our use of scarce resources. If we act as though there is only one right way of negotiating we become just as stifling as a "momma bird" teacher because the multi-valent complexities of what it means to be human are ignored.

A Common Challenge

Whenever we are given expert information that lacks an awareness of the need to reflect on how the information might inform our own personal or professional journeys and the ways we have come to contruct our realities, we risk our own hard-won personal authority. If we are not able to critically sort through the resulting cognitive dissonance, we can dogmatize what we have received. In the process of becoming shallow true believers we will regurgitate what we have learned when an occasion permits or requires. This is a dangerous position; one result being that we may also unintentionally disperse misinformation, or misinterpreted or irrelevant information—depending on how we make sense of what we have been "fed."

Responding to what Nel Noddings (1984, p. 181) calls the "crisis of caring" in our culture involves looking beyond any single way of being with young children and instead seeking historical and social perspectives out of which we can learn to care in more open and fluid ways. In the process, we will need to consider how what we are doing is profoundly political; that is, while there are a variety of good and helpful ways to teach and care for young children, each way carries political consequences. "Who benefits?" is an effective question we can use to address this dilemma. Individuals, communities, and cultures that are not afraid to be open sometimes risk developing myths out of the often unintentional distortion of facts. Such distortion may serve purposes that reside in the politics and policies of people, institutions, and cultures. And if the answer to "who benefits?" is not the children, then the myth must be questioned.

Examining Who Benefits

In her book, *Mother-Infant Bonding: A Scientific Fiction*, Diane Eyer (1992) examines the popular concept of mother/child bonding, a concept which Eyer believes reduces the necessarily complex and messy relatedness of mother-infant to a flat, individualistic, antiseptic, market-driven, and scientifically skewed image of what actually occurs. That this image is hospital-based is no accident, Eyers claims. The public policy of our modern nation was designed to encourage childbirth in hospitals. The research done to help promote the hospital as the preferred location for childbirth was disseminated in an effort to make the modern, hospital-based health-care system more attractive to pregnant women. According to Eyer, "bonding" was an image that emerged from this market-driven research and that now appears to be more fiction than fact. This deception deluded women and medical personnel into thinking that given specific procedures (such as mothers holding their babies for a set amount of time) they could guarantee an inoculation ("bonding") that would make certain the health and well-being of all infants.

Along the way, administrators who would not bow to public pressure and support funding procedures related to mother-child "bonding" were depicted as ogres and were said to be neglecting a necessary process that in some mystical way assured the future of all infants. Mothers who opted for home birth and who questioned the formality of the hospital birth process were simply discounted as uneducated and out of touch with modern science.

Eyer values the importance of parents developing a special relationship with their babies, but warns that our reliance upon scientific formulas is too easy an answer for such a complex, on-going, relational task. "Bonding" as a solution betrays our cultural assumption that only science has access to truth. This uni-vocal view is, for Eyer, "a reflection of a deeply embedded problem within our society regarding the uses of science." She warns that "Even when the research is well constructed, once the findings are used as guidelines for moral behavior, there is great danger that the results will be shaped to suit variable social and political ends." She goes on to suggest that "the greatest danger is that we have made scientists into a modern clergy." By co-opting religion's role, individuals other than scientists who might present different "truths" are eliminated from the context. "Truth" becomes objective and dispassionate. Its location is outside self and community. Eyer asserts, "The myth that researchers are objective distances them from their subjects and creates a unidirectional flow of information that restricts information to the confines of the researchers conceptions." It is clear that all research emerges in relation to such non-objective conceptions; that is, research is born in subjectiveness. Posing as objective cannot mask the fact that the researcher is subjective. It is also clear that all knowledge does not reside within the researcher; "...subjects also have expert knowledge about their own condition from their own unique standpoint" (Eyer, pp. 197–98).

As she emphasizes a multi-vocal, relational view of human relationships, Eyer advocates that children have many other people in their families and extended families. In addition they are also impacted by the food they eat, the sounds they hear, and the hopes that adults have for them. Writing about young children, she concludes:

> They have parents whose relationships are sometimes cordial and sometimes discordant, affected by worries about money, health, work and recognition. Children and their parents live in communities that are sometimes peaceful and beautiful, sometimes violent and ugly. People can connect with each other intellectually, emotionally, through daily caretaking, through games, through music and art, through formal learning and from long distances. There are many, many dimensions to the nurturance of our children. To the extent that we have reduced these processes to "bonding" we have done ourselves a disservice. To the extent that we continue to deify the maternal-child relationship, hoping it will issue us transcendence from the mundane problems of an unpredictable world, we are lost. (pp. 199–200)

Thus a presumed set of "facts" tested, analyzed, and controlled becomes a "truth"—in this case "bonding"—a doctrine that ignores the relational mystery of mother-child nurturance and in doing so gets wedded to the financial circumstances of the social institution of the hospital. Who wins? Who loses? Simply suggesting that "facts" lead to certain conclusions and then behaving, as Kelly suggests, as if such conclusions are "truth" avoids the larger relational framework within which such "facts" were generated.

As we consider Eyer's critique of what she terms the scientific myth of mother-infant bonding and the ensuing hospital policies, we must also ask if there are concepts other than "bonding" that should be investigated. Some questions that invite further study could be: "What might have been missing from events surrounding the birthing process that influenced families to embrace the so-called "fact of bonding?" "What voices were absent in the sterile hospital procedure of childbirth in the middle of the twentieth century?" "What voices aided in the propagation of the concept of "bonding" as a proven scientific fact?"

Perhaps examining another way of being with a newborn immediately following birth and the myths that inform that experience—myths we might consider "pre-modern"—will help us move further beyond what we know about this experience into what we do not yet know.

Another Way

Nolbert Kunonga (1992), a scholar from the African nation of Zimbabwe, describes a relational framework for childbirth that differs greatly from the one described by Eyer. Kunonga tells the story of his friend, Kikuyu, and her experience after the birth of her child in Kenya, her native country.

> The midwife took the child, bathed and oiled him. I took a goat, and in the presence of the whole family and some members of our village, I sacrificed it to thank the ancestors and God. My father, who was the

oldest member of our clan, took some of the meat and some water and placed them on the ground for the ancestors to join us in the meal. He told the spirits that the child was born to the community, to the spirits and to God, and that he was theirs as much as he was mine. (pp. 105–106)

The African scholar Kunonga uses his friend's story to illustrate an African principle of "existence in relation." In Kunonga's words, it illustrates "the vital relationship which the African maintains with nature, *Mwari-God*, the deities, the ancestors, the tribe, the clan, the extended family and the nuclear family" (p. 106). Such an understanding is very different from the mother-infant bonding process honored within western culture.

When we bring Kunonga's understanding of the birth of Kikuyu's child into dialogue with Eyer's scientific myth, we can begin to transcend our own mental constructs of the world into which children are "birthed." "Momma bird" unicultural procedures of describing families and what happens within families can be just as limiting as "momma bird" teaching. There is always more to be understood. Beyond the birth, families and communities have ways of maintaining a spirituality of caring.

In Kenya, Kikuyu's family and community live in near proximity even as the "belongingness" of the newborn is extended beyond human relationship. In the U.S.A. we tend to privately ground (as with Eyer's scientific myth of bonding) our babies' relationships with mother and then family. But in this country those families that claim deep religious commitment to that which is beyond the human relationship, much like Kikuyu's family and community, often also engage in formalized rituals such as baptism and circumcision in order to mark the child's belonging.

There are many feelings and different ways of being that undergird such outward signs of belonging. Because many families in the U.S.A. are so mobile, supportive systems that honor such understandings in a relational way often reach beyond the immediate community in the form of extended family networks.

Across the Miles

In the U.S.A. young children and their grandparents may live on different coasts. While their communities may differ, the sense of being family can remain intact. New parents-to-be can therefore be supported from a distance. This support depends a great deal on the resources available within a family network and the ways in which family members interpret themselves as family.

I am remembering a visit with my niece and her nine-month-old daughter in the home of my brother and his wife during one of my semi-annual trips to a place where I had once lived. As Julie came into the family room she bounced Adalie on her hip much as I had carried my own children. I was sitting on the floor looking at some recent family photos with Lois, Julie's mother. Julie handed Adalie to her mother (Adalie's grandmother and my sister-in-law) and sat down on the floor across from me. Julie, Lois, and I talked for a while as Adalie playfully crawled back and forth from her grandmother's to her mother's laps. Occasionally Adalie would look at me as she played with her mother's hair or her grandmother's shoe. After returning to Julie's lap and nestling the top of her head against Julie's cheek, Adalie stood up and reached toward me, took my hand, and then climbed into my lap. Soon she snuggled into my arms, her head leaning back on my shoulder.

I was delighted when Adalie included me among her trusted others and somewhat surprised, for I hadn't seen her since shortly after she was born. Yet, in some non-verbal way she sensed that her mother trusted me—that I was family. As a thirteen-year-old, I had carried baby Julie about, and almost fourteen years later my own daughter was given Lois' middle name as her middle name. The feelings went even deeper, for Lois had been part of my life since I was four and she was my brother's high school sweetheart. Somehow all of this engendered feelings and ways of being between Julie, Lois, and me that Adalie picked up on. Families have ways of maintaining their "family-ness," their ways of being family across miles.

Emily Nyoni, an early childhood professional from Zimbabwe, describes this "networking" of families from a different perspective. Just as Kunonga has done in relation to Kenya, Nyoni (personal communication, 1995) stresses that Zimbabwean children belong not only to the father (and for the modern Zimbabwean family, the mother as well) but to the community into which the child is born. Thus child care becomes a community concern.

The child may be sent to live with the grandparents for a period of time, which is commonly done when a child is two and there is a new baby. Other community members are uncles and cousins who act in ways that denote different family constellations from those within the U.S.A. .

When Emily Nyoni came here to study for several years, her young son remained in a rural area in Zimbabwe with her mother. While she missed both the young child and her older son who was in boarding school in Zimbabwe, she described herself as not being worried about them.

Her mother travelled by bus every two weeks to be sure her older son was safe and doing well in boarding school. Emily Nyoni's youngest son's father visited him at her mother's home every other weekend. During these visits, the father would carry the young child on his shoulders wherever he went. Family members saved memories of the children's experiences of growing to share with Nyoni. When Nyoni returned home for a visit, her youngest son, who was a baby when she left, was now three-years-old. The family had kept Emily alive in her young son's memory. He was a happy, spontaneous child, interested in exploring his world and feeling deeply connected to his family, Emily included. The older son was growing and learning as well. One of Emily Nyoni's most cherished possessions in the U.S.A. student townhouse she shared with others from her homeland was a large picture of her two sons. Emily's family networking had reached across three continents and an ocean.

four

The "S" Words

When we are with young children, we must take what we are doing seriously, for we are on sacred ground.

—Sr. Rosemary Small, OSB

The cover of an issue of *Newsweek* advertised its contents with these words: "The Search for the Sacred: America's Quest for Spiritual Meaning." Inside the magazine, journalists assured us that it was "OK, even chic to use the 'S' words—soul, sacred, spiritual, sin." Shortly after reading the article, I sat in a beautician's chair getting my hair cut and noted a colorful certificate hanging on the wall announcing that one of the shop's employees had recently attended a training session on the "Spirituality of Hair Coloring."

Scholars, too, are giving serious thought to the spiritual dimension of human development. Some years ago Robert Coles told his challenging story of six-year-old Ruby, a primary participant in the desegregation of the public schools in New Orleans. With wonder, Coles (1982) describes his life work as making sense out of how Ruby and other children transcend such circumstances. In Coles words, "Here was a little girl who was called every name in the book, who was insulted and threatened, and yet could find time in the evening to pray for the people who were heckling her" (p. 15).

This and other similar experiences with children led Coles (1990) to re-examine his research and to publish *The Spiritual Life of Children*. In his earlier article, Coles reflected, "What can you say, psychiatrically, sociologically, in terms of developmental theory, as it's put, when you have a six-year-old with that kind of attitude?" And he adds, "All you can do is be in awe of her" (1982, pp. 15–16).

More recently in the second edition of his book, *Frames of Mind*, Howard Gardner (1993) has suggested that in addition to his seven intelligences, he continues "to think that some form of 'spiritual intelligence' may well exist" (p. xviii). Gardner has kept this question open in relation to his own research.

The Present Scene

As indicated by the *Newsweek* cover, my experience in the hair salon, and the work of scholars, many definitions of "spirituality" are currently being bantered about and explored in a variety of ways. In a previous era spirituality within the western world was a term commonly connected to the Christian Church. What is notable in today's conversations about spirituality is its broad, popular usage and its frequent lack of definition or connection with any formal, religious establishment. Similarly, there is no longer a single, unified understanding of the divine; instead, voices from the margin increasingly speak of a God who is not all powerful. These voices raise questions of justice and, in the process, redefine God as having more to do with relatedness than with absoluteness (Jennings, 1995).

Such issues interest early-childhood practioners, especially because many adults regard what they do with young children as a form of ministry and their own spirituality as a necessary resource in that process. This is often a private definition; neither the church nor the profession encourages much conversation in this area, assuming that church-state separation closes discussion. Nevertheless, such concerns emerge as people try to bridge a deep spirituality and an in-depth knowledge of child development. One such voice is that of Marian McKinney, a master teacher of young children in a second-grade classroom in the Chicago Public Schools.

Marian's Story as a Young Child

1968 is a year that for me encapsulates many traumatic experiences. My most poignant memory was the sudden (early) dismissal from school on April 4, 1968. There were crowds, crying and screaming. One of the older students grabbed my hand and led me to safety. We rode home frightened and crouched on the floor of Mrs. Marcie's station wagon, unaware of the rioting just one block south of our small Lutheran day school.

The next morning as we rode to school we saw the shattered, scattered glass in the streets and on the sidewalk. We saw the boarded up and burned buildings. Mrs. Marcie could have chosen another route to school, but she didn't. I think she wanted us to see. We spoke in hushed voices about what it all meant and we talked about the sad faces of Yolanda, Martin III, Dexter and Bernice. Mrs. Marcie just listened.

The previous spring, the death of my favorite uncle, Joe, taught me one of life's most stinging realities—the permanence of death. But the assassination of Martin Luther King was different. We grieved as a community. I already knew that we were not free, but I learned that sometimes the price we pay for engaging in the struggle is death. I also understood that I was expected to engage in that same struggle, and moreover I wanted to.

Death was a recurring theme in 1968. Our neighbor, Mrs. Manning, the mother of two of my playmates, died. A fatal accident during the construction of the Dan Ryan Highway claimed the father of a classmate. My favorite cousins lost their mother. Cousin Caromey, the eldest grandchild, was funeralized on my sixth birthday, December 6, 1968. He broke his neck playing football. After being confined to a wheelchair, he died a few months later. His black wheelchair stored in the family basement served as an awful reminder of his fate.

It seemed to me that death knew my address, at the very least, my street name. Death was too close to home—literally. I knew the difference between reality and fantasy: now reality was the more frightening.

My fear of death was only eclipsed by fear for my personal safety. 1968 was the year I transferred from the small Lutheran school where I completed kindergarten to the large neighborhood public school. Gone were the comforts of Mrs. Marcie's station wagon. It was an eight block walk. No more Matin Service, music, and no more "God talk." There seemed to be fights at the new school everyday; something Pastor never tolerated.

My "loci of control" diminished. My vocabulary continued to expand: "Black Panthers," "white flight," "gangs," "politics," "recruit," "campaign," "integration," "prejudice," plus the latest slang and the introduction to a few swear words. I was dehumanized as my body was now reduced to the sum of its parts—"Pussy," as in give me some p ... ; "tiddies," as in "she let him feel her t ... ;" "butt", as in "I'm going to kick your b. ..." My frightened eyes and my unwillingness to fight back (or even talk back) made me an easy target.

Adults referred to me as "the little girl that never smiled." Some went a step further calling me a "mean little girl." Some accepted my countenance as a personal challenge. These were the adults that made funny faces, tugged at my fat cheeks, tickled my chin, or asked intrusive and embarrassing questions. Other adults simply *demanded* that I smile. Few took time to *ask me* about me—my hopes, my fears, my dreams. Few listened when I tried to tell them.

Nightly prayers only exacerbated the situation. "Now I lay me down to sleep, I pray the Lord my soul to keep. *If I should die before I wake,* I pray the Lord my soul to take."

I didn't like that prayer, in fact I hated it. And after all I'd been through, understandably, I had difficulty securing a good night's sleep. There were nightmares, episodes of bed-wetting, a small amount of crying, and a lot of questions, especially at bed time. Bed time seemed to me my preferred time for "God talk," but I stopped asking questions because nobody could answer them. I learned not to cry because it made people angry.

I have worked in the public school system for almost ten years. I have a Master's degree in Curriculum, Teaching, and Psychological Studies. I am well versed in the theories of cognitive development. The theories of Jean Piaget tell me that at that young age I should have been unable to cogitate on things theological or process my own pain or challenge authority by exercising my right to free speech. Piaget told me that I should have been unable to relate or emphasize with human suffering; I also should have been unable to possess a global perspective or own a liberation theology. . . . But by age five I already recognized that my Nia (personal power, as defined in the African American value system) came from God.

As she ended this reflective piece on her childhood, Marian McKinney was determined to include those children she now teaches in Chicago. The words she decided to use deeply reflect her spirituality of caring:

When I cried for you, I visited my own pain. They may separate church from state, but they will never separate us from the love of God.

Are the "S" Words Really "OK"?

Marian McKinney clearly identifies the separation of church and state as one of the challenges that faces those of us who work in the public sector, particularly if we consider the spiritual life of young children and of ourselves important to such work. It is clear that even though she recognizes the separation of church and state, McKinney also understands God to be present in her relationship with her young charges. She knows that the tension inherent in this position could get her into trouble.

As indicated by *Newsweek*, it may be "OK" to use the "S" words, but using religious language in the secular world when employed by public agencies and paid through public funds is not allowed. Within the public arena, we have kept our distance from identifying with the particularities of anything that might be understood as being sectarian or religiously divisive. This circumstance has a long history. The separation of church and state is clearly spelled out in our constitution.

Our Constitution

For a long time our country has proceeded as if everyone shared a common faith, a common way of naming an ultimate concern from which we as a nation drew strength. As a people the citizens of the U.S.A. understood they were free to worship God as they pleased because separation of church and state lay at the heart of our constitution. The underlying assumption is that we would worship a higher being (God), but we did not all have to do it in the same way.

The authors of our constitution viewed religion as so powerful and important that the task of teaching the formal words, symbols, and principles of faith to children should be the responsibility of individual families and communities. The constitution, therefore, assured citizens the right of freedom of religion. This meant that no one could stop them from worshiping according to their religious beliefs. Such a stance came out of a long history of persecution and served to allay fears of those who fled such persecution by letting them know that they could not be punished for their religious beliefs in the new country.

As Stephen L. Carter (1994) reminds us in *The Culture of Disbelief*, The First Amendment to the Constitution of the United States of America begins with the words "Congress shall make no law respecting an establishment of religion . . . " and is followed by, "or prohibiting the free exercise thereof." The intent was to establish religious liberty, not to somehow save the state from religion. Yet we operate today as if the "saving" of the state from religion is paramount. Perhaps, as Carter suggests, this is neither helpful nor faithful to the authors of the Constitution. Certainly this position is a familiar one to those who teach and care for young children; yet, it has been coupled with a second position that is almost as universally accepted by professors of child development. Deep within the literature that informs research and policy related to children and families in our country lies the contribution of Freud, which exacerbates the idea that we must save our citizens from religion.

Impact of Freud

Within our existing child development theories there is a reluctance (if not an aversion) to address the spiritual dimension of development. This has roots in Freud's rejection of anything that has to do with organized religion.

More recently, Heinz Kohut (1985) built a psychoanalytic theory with more tolerance for religion's supportive aspect. In relation to Freud, Kohut suggested that "religion constitutes a set of cultural values that he [Freud] totally underestimated: there was no opening in his system for such things" (p. 261). While Kohut's insights provide a helpful direction and while not all child development theories are psychoanalytic, Freud's impact on the field remains considerable. There is, however, a third dynamic that muddies our ability within the U.S.A. to address spirituality in our public discourse.

Uniculturalism

From the time of the inception of Horace Mann's public school movement until the 1960s, the accepted "religious strategy" of the nation and of the church was that children would receive home and church instruction related to their families' religious beliefs while they attended the common school that taught the progressive vision that would teach them how to be modern citizens. This seemed to work well, at least on a superficial level, as long as the country was viewed as universally sharing the dominant Protestant values out of which Horace Mann had "fathered" the tax supported public school.

Yet, educators such as John Dewey knew that one could not separate the spiritual component of life from a whole child perspective on education. Thus in his book *A Common Faith*, Dewey (1934) makes a distinction between the terms "religious" and "religion."

For Dewey, "religion" is the formal expression (words, symbols, and dogma) of a specific community's system of beliefs, while the "religious" describes the universal experience underlying such words and other symbols. Dewey's school would connect with and be grounded in this universal experience and would prepare students for participation in democracy. He suggests that as a nation we share "a common faith" that undergirds our sense of being a democratic community. In commenting on Dewey, Alan Ryan suggests that "since democracy was for him more a matter of culture than of politics, faith in a democratic society must be faith in a common culture" (Ryan, 1995, p. 172). The way Dewey chose to understand the role of the school was as the "common faith" of a democratic society tested by a rising tide of immigration, labor disputes—indeed, all the anxieties of his era.

Like Horace Mann, Dewey held a unicultural view of society with its accompanying Protestant Judeo-Christian values. In Kenneth Wilbur's words, that culture appeared to be dominated by "a mixture of mythic Protestant ethic and

American nationalistic immortality symbols" (1983, p. 81). Such symbols clearly were meant to be expressions of a common faith and organizing ethos, and were commonplace in the morning rituals of the public school well into the 60s. In 1961, as I prepared for teacher certification in Slippery Rock, Pennsylvania, I recorded the following observation in a kindergarten:

> The teacher sits on a chair facing the half circle of 25 young children. One other child sits on a child-size chair positioned next to the teacher's chair. This child holds a small American flag in her right hand which rests in her lap. The back of each child appears ramrod straight, feet are firmly planted on the floor and hands rest in laps as the teacher reads the prescribed number of verses from the King James version of the protestant *Bible*. Small heads nod, arms and legs wiggle; yet, the tiny bottoms sit squarely in the bright blue chairs as if glued there.
>
> When it is time for the recitation of the protestant version of the Lord's Prayer, hands are folded and heads bowed. From time to time brown and blue eyes peek through the fingers of the folded hands as tiny lips mouth the children's perceptions of the words of the prayer along with the teacher.
>
> After the prayer comes the Pledge of Allegiance to the flag, a task which takes considerable time getting underway since placing the right hand over the heart appears to be a challenge for some of the five-year-olds. The pledge complete, the children hesitantly sing, "Three cheers for the red, white and blue. . ." The child positioned next to the teacher waves the small flag as if her hand is fashioned from wood.

Cultural Diversity Recognized

It was not long after I wrote the above observation that the requirement of protestant *Bible* readings and prayers in public schools was challenged in our courts. As John Elias (1991) suggests, "It seemed at that time that the U.S. had finally become enveloped in the secularization process according to which society and its institutions achieved full autonomy from the religious realm and were free to pursue their objectives without religious influence" (p. 456).

Today religious language is consigned to religious institutions. Because such language often is the language used in discussions of spirituality, there is no place in the public sector to use what *Newsweek* terms the "S" words—"soul, sacred, spiritual, sin." Such words remain inappropriate in conversations regarding education and public policy.

Stalled Public Discourse

Recently, a group of practitioners, administrators, parents, and people involved in various ways with public policy met at the University of Chicago to explore ways to deal with the violence and injustice that many of our young children live with on a daily basis. As a group of about one-hundred-and-fifty, we listened to several speakers and then were dispersed into small groups to address compelling issues.

The group in which I found myself was charged with discussing school and community relationships. We readily agreed upon an impressive list of activities which were written on large sheets of paper and hung on the wall as a focus for further discussion. In my notebook I recorded the final list of proposed activities generated:

- The creation of a comprehensive community plan that reflects the values of individual communities

- The design of strategic aspects of any plans that might be developed to insure broad involvement and a common vision
- The involvement of business
- Forging school/community partnerships for creative school and community programs
- Nurturing trusting relationships between adults and children

Consensus on these recommendations came quickly and without much conflict. What did not come easily but which brought a great deal of conflict was the introductory statement to our list. Several members of the small group I was in had suggested we precede the listing of activities with: "Creating public and private spaces that allow spirituality, principles, ethics and virtues to be developed and to be nurtured."

The words 'principles, ethics and virtues" were viewed as acceptable, but the word "spirituality" became the subject of controversy; the following comments were vehemently made:

> "If you're talking about community, spirituality must be included," said one participant.

> "The separation of church and state rules out such talk in public-funded programs," argued a woman with arms tightly folded across her chest. "To do so disregards our constitution."

> "Spirituality is inappropriate and irrelevant," said another.

> One public leader worried, "We might be misunder-

stood and relegated to the far right if spirituality is included in our proposal." He quickly added, "It's not that I don't think spirituality is important, it is. But using the word can be politically dangerous."

At points the debate within this group became heated over the inclusion of that single word, "spirituality." When consensus broke down, the group called for a vote. By a simple majority the group decided that the word "spirituality" would be omitted.

I left the group wondering how whatever it was that people construed as spirituality could be discussed if the word could not be used. How could any discussion of spirituality be put away on a metaphorical shelf and stamped "dangerous stuff never to be examined in the public arena?" I also came away amazed by the power of the word. If such a word is so powerful, can it simply be cut out of the discussion of what it is that schools and communities do?

A New World in an Old Place

As I end this chapter, I realize that I am not satisfied with answers that relegate spirituality to the private sphere or those that categorize it exclusively as a component of organized religion. My concern is the whole child. To suggest that spirituality is not an appropriate topic for public discourse about children seems shortsighted, particularly since the richness of such conversation (especially when a variety of cultural voices are engaged) often provides a sense of hopefulness for our future.

We have to look at familiar ground in a new way in order to address issues of spirit, spirituality, and spiritual development in the secular worlds in which our young children spend so much time. Perhaps we can learn something from

Will Watterson, the cartoonist who draws "Calvin and Hobbes," two figures aptly named for a theologian and a philosopher.

In the last regular Sunday cartoon drawn by Watterson, the cartoonist contemplates what might face Calvin and Hobbes as he takes a break from drawing them in syndicated newspapers. It is intresting that Watterson draws his "final" cartoon with Calvin and Hobbes set on exploring an old field from a new perspective:

> Calvin pushes his way through newly fallen snow on a bright January day. Snowdrifts almost reach his waist as he plows forward into a large, snow covered field. Faithful tiger Hobbes walks in Calvin's track, carrying a toboggan. Calvin exclaims, "Wow, it really snowed last night! Isn't it wonderful?"
>
> Waking to the excitement of the experience, Hobbes brightens. Catching snowflakes with his extended paws, he suggests "It's like having a big white sheet of paper to draw on!"
>
> All that is familiar is covered with snow and the world appears "brand new." There is a freshness in the air as Calvin concludes, "It's a magical world."
>
> Together Calvin and Hobbs climb on the toboggan and push off down a slope. The little cloud of words over Calvin's head reads, "Let's go exploring!"

There may be trees to dodge, drifts to tumble into, and hidden rocks that will slow the discussion of spirituality down, but like Watterson (and Calvin and Hobbes), we can make a conscious choice to explore old places in new ways. The potential richness and practical implication of such an exploration for a whole child approach to child development—including the possible relevance of a spirituality of caring—demands an extended forum for such conversation. Thus it becomes essential that we ourselves critically reflect what we mean by the "S" words and then "spiritedly" enter the arenas where decisions affecting young children are made, affirming that advocates for the welfare of children cannot dismiss such an important dynamic without further discussion. It is to that task that I now turn.

five

A Spirituality of Caring

... we meet as human beings who have much in common: a heart, a face, a voice, the presence of a soul, fear, hope, the ability to trust, a capacity for compassion and understanding, the kinship of being human.

—*Abraham Joshua Heschel*

It is a sunny spring day in a state-funded early-childhood program on the south side of Chicago. Deneita Jo Farmer, the teacher of a group of four- and five-year-olds, helps some children choose plants for their brightly painted clay planters that are the results of several days of considerable planning and work. A mother holding a five-month-old baby settles into a rocking chair nearby. An assistant teacher observes as several children build with blocks and others explore the habits of the resident guinea pigs. Out on the playground an assistant teacher and another parent guide a group of kite builders who paint a large kite and several smaller ones—the fruits of a week's work.

Inside the classroom one of the young planters is Spanish-speaking, one is bi-lingual, and two others speak only English.

When the group gets stuck trying to figure out the Spanish word for one of the plants, the teacher asks the bi-lingual assistant for help. The assistant gives several translations and then suggests they check the English to Spanish dictionaries on the classroom bookshelves. One of the children gets a large dictionary. As the teacher looks up the word, the children lean expectantly over the book. After the proper word is found and discussed at length, the teacher prints with great care the English and the Spanish words on a card and then tapes the card on the wall near where they are working.

Suddenly the door from the playground bursts open and the assistant teacher enters with Maria, who has paint and tears running down her face. Napolena is also in tow, still gripping a paint brush and the brush is dripping paint. The teacher listens as the assistant describes Napolena's streaking of Maria's face with paint.

With an arm around each child the teacher guides them to the classroom sink. "Come, let's help Maria wash the paint off her face," she says to Napolena and the small group of children who have gathered at the door.

The bi-lingual assistant teacher positions herself immediately behind the child, Maria, while facing the teacher and translating her words into Spanish for Maria. Maria begins crying loudly at this point. The assistant also helps to clarify the words that accompany Maria's sobs (It is as if we are watching a well choreographed dance of communication as Spanish is translated into English and English into Spanish, the assistant teacher's translation just seconds behind the words of the teacher and the children, yet in sync with the strong feelings the event engenders).

The teacher helps Napolena wash the paint from Maria's face and holds a mirror so both children can see. The teacher talks with the painter and the painted about the misunderstanding leading to the present moment and about the feelings all of them are experiencing, including herself. Using a warm damp cloth brought by one of the other children, she carefully wipes Maria's face as Napolena nestles against the teacher's shoulder.

A Spirituality of Caring

Napolena, Maria, their friends, and the caring adults present are learning a great deal on this sunny spring day. "Spirit" is plentiful and present in all participants for they are all open to new experiences.

The terms "spirit" and "spirituality" give us a way to talk about the dynamics of development in Deneita Jo Farmer's classroom—the spirit present within the children and an understanding of spirituality as that which surrounds and flows through the children, families, communities, and extended networks of caring others. Yet, using the term "spirituality" and its root word "spirit" in relation to an early-childhood center located in a school setting in the secular arena does entail some risk-taking. In addition to the possibility of being banished to the politically far right or viewed as behaving in ways that are unconstitutional, these words can be misconstrued to suggest an eerie world of ghosts existing in a reality beyond our own.

It is not my intent, nor my aim to fall into the trap suggested by Mary Wolff-Salin (1986) of using sets of dichotomies such as body/spirit or spiritualistic/materialistic. "Spirit" is that property of being fully and wholly human that fuels our predisposition to transcend each and every condition in our experience. "Spirituality" is a construction of meaning meant to inform the human way we engage in that process of transcendence. Margaret Chatterjee (1989) appropriately suggests that "there can be no spirituality shorn of community" (p. 6). A spirituality of caring is a way of naming what it is we do as a community to nurture and educate spirited young children for the invitations to transcendence presented by life; this is a human activity performed by and for whole people in a whole community. Children are whole people and so are we. As Erikson (1964) emphasizes, "whole children need a whole world to be whole in" (p. 136).

Splitting children into numerous unconnected components needs to be seen for what it is—a metaphorical and cultural perspective. We exist within culturally approved constructions of reality. We take part in compartmentalization both in relation to human development, and in the ways we approach and understand our westernized institutions. We primarily attend schools to learn and contact social services agencies to deal with problems related to everyday living. Churches, synagogues, and temples provide a space for the worship of the source of ultimate value and power as it has been socially constructed and named in our faith communities. Hospitals take care of our wounded and suffering bodies and minds. Yet we take all of our being and all of the ways we make sense out of our reality into these various institutions, and what happens in any one of them is complex and related to what happens in the others.

We are not compartmentalized people nor are our youngest children. If we understand spirituality as the way we ascribe meaning to the deeper level of existence that surrounds us and is in us and our relationships, then we cannot lock spirituality out of any institution that wants to do what is culturally expected—teach, heal, help, serve.

The planet we share is a small one. The very existence of young children in our lives necessitates that we care for them until they can care for themselves and those who are important to them. If we place any of our children in danger, we place all of our children and ourselves in danger. When

we care about our youngest children, any institution involved in their lives must be challenged to enter into a spirituality of caring if it is to become, or remain, a shared
center of value and power within the context of our communities. When such identification occurs, a particular language of meaning emerges. In other words, the communal
network of values, people, ideas, and institutions provides
a contextual location for understanding concepts related to
the spirit. While such contexts are not interchangeable, we
do translate, within our communities, the meaning of spirituality for children as they learn through active participation with others. We—through actions and words—
communicate our perceptions of important events and
ways of doing things, including our values and ideas about
power. And so, a spirituality focused on caring provides
shared relational contexts which focus and permeate the
horizons of our experiences with young children.

Core Conditions Toward a Spirituality of Caring

A spirituality of caring, then, can be described as the
shared construct of those within a given community who
support, nurture, guide, teach, and learn in caring, hopeful
ways. A core condition can be defined as something that is
fundamental to this understanding. There are four such
core conditions in a spirituality of caring: (1) the provision
of hospitable space; (2) the acceptance, embracing, and
providing of experiences; (3) the presence of authentic, caring adults; and (4) an affirmation of the process of learning ... of being able to spiritedly transcend present
conditions (Myers and Myers, 1992).

The Provision of Hospitable Space

The first of these core conditions involves hospitality.
Deneita Jo Farmer, the teacher mentioned earlier and her staff

on the south side of Chicago are providing hospitable space in a state-funded preschool. The idea of hospitable space is borrowed from Henri Nouwen (1975) who, writing within the Christian tradition, claims it "is our vocation to convert the hostis into hospes (Greek words)." This is to say that our work as humans is to convert the "enemy into a guest and to create the free and fearless space where brotherhood and sisterhood can be formed and fully experienced" (p. 46).

Practicing hospitality for the adults in Deneita Jo Farmer's preschool setting means helping Napolena (the painter) wash Maria's face (the painted) so that each child might feel a welcome part of the classroom community. The assistant teacher who speaks Maria's language becomes involved in a dance of communication as the two women work together as a team to provide words to help the children sort out feelings of confusion, frustration, and anger. Hospitable space is there not only for Maria and Napolena, but for the other children and the visiting parent and baby as well. In Nouwen's words, this classroom is a place where "brotherhood and sisterhood" are in the process of being "formed and fully experienced."

The Importance of Experience

The many faces of experience are the second core condition of a spirituality of caring. Children's behavior and activities take place within the contextual reality of their lives. Such contextuality can be denied if teachers follow only a prescribed curriculum and avoid the strong feelings associated with the events of a child's life. Children not only bring experiences into the classroom, they also have experiences within the classroom. What do adults in the lives of young children do in situations like the painter and painted event? Someone not able to be fully present in such an experience might retreat in fear or try to control the situation. But in this instance, Napolena and Maria's teachers built a curriculum of caring out of the spontaneous events. When a word was needed they searched for it. When paint covered a tiny face, the painter and the painted were helped to deal with the paint and the feelings engendered. This is not to suggest that anything goes or that anyone can do this task. It is to suggest that the event and the teacher's sensitive intervention is the content of a curriculum of caring that intentionally engages the experiences of young children.

Deneita Jo Farmer is an exemplary early-childhood educator who brings a strong background in the field of child development, years of professional early-childhood preparation, educational experience, and a strong professional ethic to her work with young children and their families. Building on the knowledge of her profession, she is competently applying development theory, research, and professional practice to a classroom environment in which children's life experiences are taken seriously. Farmer ensures that there is plenty of physical and emotional room in her classroom for the world that comes to school with the children as well as the experiences they have while there.

Presence

Deneita Jo Farmer builds a sense of community among the adults in her classroom that allows them to act as adults; that is, ensure safety, model communicative behavior, and provide a steady, reliable structure for each day. They also know each child well and interact with children in a nurturing, caring way. It is not enough that the adults are simply in the classroom. They must connect with the children, and take seriously the importance ascribed to the verbal and non-verbal communication of each one.

The third core condition is the presence of caring, resourceful, and challenging adults—people who can be strong presences in the child's experiences. Young children often see these adults as standing with them in both tough and joyful times.

As colleagues, they model cooperative behavior, help the children name strong feelings and identify and solve problems. A caring adult presence in the classroom proves to children that they are being heard, seen, and responded to in meaningful ways. Such adults know that children do not compartmentalize the events of their lives, putting a part of who they are in a box and then shoving it under a bed in order to come to preschool. Everything that they are comes to preschool with them. Never reducing children to objects, a caring adult is able to recognize the inherent value and worth of each child, while offering the child the unique chacteristics, strengths, and capabilities the adult possesses.

In a spirituality of caring, presence includes the relational, dialogical connection described in Chapter One. Presence is a meeting of spirit and all that implies. As adults who are present for young children, we relish encounters like the "painter and the painted" described above. We would not want to avoid or over-control such moments, but rather embrace them in fully present ways.

But there is more that happened that day in Maria and Napolena's classroom. The fourth core condition for a spirituality of caring is that of recognizing and affirming the dynamic of transcendence; i.e. the assuredness that children can move beyond what they already know, and so can we.

The Ability to Learn: Transcending in Hope

Transcendence is the word used by Phenix (1974) to suggest that all of learning involves moving from what is known toward what is not yet known. For Phenix this movement is an underlying dynamic of the universe. Without such a dynamic, there would be no hope because things would be perceived as static with no possibility for change. By being able to transcend, a person can grow and envision a horizon without limits. To engage in the process of transcendence in order to actualize that hope is to embark on the journey of learning.

In Maria and Napolena's classroom, the entire staff is informed by a sense that languages can be used for communication and that strong feelings can be transcended. It is in this hospitable space that caring presences learn, listen, care for, and begin to understand the behaviors and feelings present in everyone—children and adults—in the classroom. Children come to trust in such presences and in themselves and thus move from what they know to what they don't yet know. Rather than saying, "That's the way life is, people speak different languages and can't understand one another; people throw paint and hurt one another and we can't do anything different," this particular caring community together affirmed the hope-filled dynamic of transcendence and moved forward into new experiences. If our young children are to thrive, they must all have similar opportunities to flourish.

Teaching as Deneita Jo Farmer does touches the raw feelings of being human. She, members of her staff, and parents of the center's children all work together to help young children recognize the sensations of feelings. Their own spirituality of caring allows them to guide the children and in the process both adults and children assign meaning to and name their feelings as they continue to develop life-enhancing ways of being together. Such occasions of transcendence have implications for the global community. Put simply, these four core conditions must be present in any good day for young children anywhere. The value judgement implied by the use of the adjective "good" is intentional.

Our Challenge

In their book *Within our Reach: Breaking the Cycle of Disadvantage*, Lisbeth and Daniel Schorr (1988) state that we know how to deal with the challenges that young children face if we want them to grow into adults who can care for themselves and for those whom they love. But we often fail, perhaps because as Henry Giroux (1992) suggests, we are not willing to unlearn our own privilege. If we are concerned about helping our culture (and our children) become more caring, we need to recognize and see beyond our own advantage (while maintaining an authentic voice) in order to demystify and make visible the ways in which knowledge becomes "encased in historical and institutional structures that both privilege and exclude particular readings, voices, aesthetics, authority, representations, and forms of society" (p. 27).

Giroux further suggests that by taking the "subject" position in a situation (here is my location; this is my voice), we as cultural workers cannot afford to fall back into defensive, binary positions ("them" vs. "us") but instead must struggle to become "border crossers" capable of hearing and understanding alternative ways of naming what is important. By doing this, Giroux suggests border crossings will allow us to embrace the richness inherent in different cultural codes, experiences, and languages.

I take Giroux's thesis seriously throughout this volume. Traditional, formal religions and the classical developmental theorists have taken great pains not to step on each others' toes. Each group has occupied a certain territory, and "border crossing" was not encouraged. It is clear that the work on either side has been rich, evocative, and replete with insights, and could provide helpful direction were we to step across the imaginary borders constructed by our disciplines.

The core conditions suggested here—(1) hospitable space; (2) centrality of experience; (3) presence; and (4) hopeful transcendence as expectation—metaphorically move us in the direction of what we know is needed to deal with the challenges young children face.

Such naming is important, but further steps must be taken. What might occur if we were to invite multiple voices into an intersubjective space where we actively crossed borders and co-constructed knowledge? Such a multi-voiced co-construction is a challenge for those of us accustomed to operating within the privilege of our own camp. What would happen if such "border crossing" became an occasion for listening? This is not to suggest that we withhold or muffle our own voice, but it is to say that even as we share our own understandings, we must be open to the discovery of further insights and questions from voices and actions other than our own. And, given such exploration, we may also choose to change some of our own deeply held beliefs about the nature of children, our roles and the roles of the institutions that affect children's lives, the nature of learning, the meaning of education, and the place of community in the lives of young children. These possibilities illustrate why, in my view, border-crossing is essential if we care about the lives of our youngest children and the world which we will leave for them.

six

Moving Beyond the Known

Someday maybe there will exist a well informed, well considered and yet fervent conviction that the most deadly of all sins is the mutilation of a child's spirit.

—*Erik H. Erikson*

Five-year-old Pernell Andre Decker adds a final stroke of blue crayon to a picture he has been working on for at least ten minutes. Calling to a nearby teacher he tells her, "Put my name here, all of it!"

Intently he watches as his teacher begins at the top left corner of his paper and carefully prints "Pernell Andre Decker." Then, using each of the crayons in the box, he painstakingly colors around his newly lettered name, taking care not to cover up any of the letters. When he returns the last crayon to the container, he announces for all to hear, "I'm Pernell Andre Decker, ain't nobody gonna tell me no different!"

When I recorded this observation in a Head Start Program on the north side of Pittsburgh, I knew that Pernell

Andre Decker was on his way to being a person who would someday be able to care for himself and others. He was well into the process of becoming a reader and a writer. He was continuing to learn that he was a person of worth—someone who could impact his environment and control his own strong feelings. He was learning that letters written respectfully by his teacher had meaning for both of them, that people used written symbols to tell each other important things, and that what he had to say was important to others. My hope was that Pernell would continue to get support for his growth.

Relationships with Self and Other

In the year-and-a-half he spent in a Head Start Program, Pernell grew from a despondent and then disruptive child to one who competently used the resources the early-childhood center had to offer. He built stores with aisles, garages with parking spaces, and sometimes a zoo with lots of cages for rubber giraffes, elephants, and tigers. Rather than dumping puzzles on the table and racing toward the exit, as he had done at one point in his development, he would look over a young friend's shoulder and point to where a piece might fit.

A critical component of the Head Start Program was the relationship between the staff and Pernell Andre's mother, Toinita. A twenty-two-year-old single mother, she had two daughters that were younger than Pernell Andre. About the time that Pernell Andre Decker colored around his printed name, Toinita was preparing to take her high school G.E.D. exam.

When she first visited the Head Start Center more than a year-and-a-half earlier with Pernell and his little sister in tow, she talked of her concern about her son. She described him as a puzzling little boy who could be seen sitting quietly a great deal of the time. As she put it, "He just seems downhearted." She described herself as really becoming concerned when she noticed him "biting at the top of his own hand."

During an initial home visit as part of Pernell Andre's entrance into the program, the head teacher from his classroom and the Head Start Program's social worker noted that he lived with his little sister, an aunt who was slightly older than Pernell Andre, and two little girls of about three and four who were cousins. During the teacher's and social worker's visit, all five children sat quietly on the worn sofa in a small scarcely furnished room. The young children were neither verbal nor physically active. There was no sign of the explosive little boy who, one month later, would race about the center, pushing play materials off shelves and children off bicycles, and send another child to the emergency room with teeth marks in her shoulder.

Figuring It Out

When his mother and sister first came with him to the center, Pernell Andre sat in a chair near the front door beside Toinita. His little sister sat in his mother's lap or wandered around the immediate area, often resting her body against Toinita. Pernell Andre watched as the other children played. When his mother would leave for a brief period of time, he would stand near the teacher or wander around the area of the large playroom near the door. When his mother returned he would again sit in the chair nearest her.

Toinita and the teacher let Pernell Andre know when Toinita was going to leave, and that she would be back for him. During Toinita's initial brief absence, the teacher would talk about what Pernell Andre's mother was doing and that she would return soon. Whenever he went to the door the teacher reminded him that his mother was coming back to take him home.

As Pernell Andre became engaged in activities and moved out into the center of the room, his mother spent longer and longer periods of time in the parent center across the hallway. Occasionally Pernell Andre would ask for his mother and go with a staff member over to the parent room and see his mother, but after spending a few minutes with her, he wanted to go back to his own room where the four-year-old children were involved in activities that interested him more than the activities in the parent room.

In the parent center, Toinita shared concerns about her young children and her inability to care for them on her own. Pregnant with her third child, she became interested in some of the community programs for herself that the Head Start staff helped her access. She enrolled her daughter in a parent/toddler program that met three mornings a week.

When Pernell Andre's behavior suddenly began to erupt into periods of explosions in his preschool classroom, Toinita informed his teachers that such explosions were also happening at home. When his grandmother, Ollie Olds, came, with his mother, to a parent meeting, Mrs. Olds said that she was glad to see that Pernell had some life in him. Toinita nodded her head in agreement.

The teachers let Toinita know that often the next step for a child who seemed to have withdrawn from interactions with others (when in hospitable space with caring adult presences) was to behave in ways that seemed to be aggressive. The teacher mentioned that even though he never put his feelings into words, he might be letting his family and teachers know that he didn't understand how to interact with others or that such interactions were even possible for him. The teachers also suggested that Pernell might be feeling overwhelmed by all of the choices in the center, and also by the other children's actions. The social worker who led activities in the parent center added that perhaps while Toinita wanted Pernell Andre to be with other children—especially little boys—and have experiences with them that she could not provide for him on her own, he might not see it that way. He might wonder, "How come she leaves me here and takes little sister with her?" His question might be a simple, yet complex, "Why am I being dumped?"

Grandmother Ollie Olds added that in addition to experiencing the new place, new people, and new things, Pernell Andre spent most of his time at home with little girls like his cousins and aunts. He was not used to being in a classroom with a group of boys. "Maybe," Ollie Olds suggested, "he's figuring out there are other little mans, too."

There was a lot to learn for a young boy who had only three-and-a-half years of life behind him. The mother, grandmother, teacher, and social worker were determined to work together to figure out what Pernell Andre did not know so that they could plan ways of teaching him how to get along both at home and in the Head Start Center. Together they asked, "What's the next step we want Pernell Andre to take?"; and, "How can we help him take it?" Implicit in their planning was a sense that Pernell Andre could learn and so could they.

Their conversations were value laden, and it soon became clear that conflictual beliefs about the appropriate roles of adults in the lives of young children were present and needed to be respected and discussed. Interchange on a number of levels involved the adults in Pernell Andre's life making joint decisions about appropriate activities for children. Once begun, decisions also had to be made regarding the roles of the various adults and community institutions in his life as well as what it meant for him to learn.

As Ollie Olds expected and the teacher and social worker confirmed, Pernell Andre's explosive behavior—with a great deal of consistent guidance on the part of the center's staff and his mother and grandmother—began to be appropriately channeled into spontaneous play activities and classroom routines. Working together, the adults in his world provided the help he needed to begin to make sense out of his own feelings and all of the information he was receiving from others in his wide-ranging environment. For a while, during his mother's early absences, he had the additional on-going presence of a staff member who helped him name and use his strong feelings in ways that were not destructive to himself, others, or the playroom's materials and equipment. Over the next several months, this staff member also helped him develop strategies for entering play situations with other children and sustaining interactions with them.

Pernell Andre gradually was becoming part of the classroom even as he discovered his own impact on that community. Together the adults in his life became invested in building Pernell Andre's sense of self within his community; this meant holding him when he hurt (emotionally and physically); seeing that he got adequate rest and food; helping him cope with difficult times; helping him figure out ways of addressing confusing issues and challenges; and, sharing their delight in his discovery, joy in learning, and pleasure in the development of his newly developed skills.

Maintenance tasks were also part of the staff's and family's focus. Such caring tasks included things like tying shoes, wiping a nose, defining limits, zipping a fly (when the zipper sticks), and buttoning buttons; this was often a relational occasion even as Pernell Andre gradually learned to do these things for himself. The adults who were engaged in the transitions of Pernell Andre's world were also a part of the regular, common rituals of his everyday life.

Ritual As Meeting Place

As the rituals that were part of coming and going, eating and sleeping, playing, toileting, greeting, and saying good bye both at home and in the center began to occur in a regular, participatory way, Pernell Andre was better able to order his own experiences. The regular, recurring nature of such rituals told him where he was in his day and what was coming next so that he could meet the expectations of those he cared about and himself. While there was an expectancy and a sameness about the rituals, there was also a newness, a relatedness, and a never-ending openness that invited him to share the "stuff" of his life.

Examining the relevance of rituals in the everyday life of young children, like Pernell Andre, and the significance of these rituals for adults in the context of religious experience provides another way to talk about spirituality within the public arena. What anthropologists and theologians term "ritual process" can help bridge the languages of professional early-childhood practice, child development, and religion. This will lead to a deeper understanding of the dynamics at work in "transcendence." Whether or not we use the "S" words in the secular world, such a discussion can moved us toward a shared meaning of spirituality.

The theologian Theodore Jennings (1982), building on the work of Victor Turner, describes a ritual as being "above all a pattern of action" (p. 111). Within ritual process, the human senses often serve as gateways into liminal space. Eating, sleeping, playing, toileting, and saying "hello" and "good-bye" are often occasioned by adults who provide materials that invoke such process. Bread, milk, crackers, cheese, and juice can be used to invoke the ritual space of a meal. By so invoking, adults are expected to steward such space, that is, to make certain that no one gets hurt at mealtime and that certain patterns of eating together are followed. Food is not thrown at mealtime, and the food that is served is safe food (it will not harm or kill you). And when meal time is invoked and the boundaries are secure, liminal space can occur.

Liminal suggests an up in the air expectation of important change occuring—i.e. that a meal is more than a meal
(in that one can be changed by what takes place during this
meal). A "meal" implies relationality and suggests that a
young child exists in large part within such relationality;
and, while not able to abstract what has occured during a
given meal, a child knows that meals imply more than a simple transaction of food.

Rituals, therefore, both structure and order experience
while making a sense of "up-in-the airness" regarding what
is known. Rituals have functions of conservation and transformation; that is, they ceremonially preserve certain patterns even as they provide occasions in which the
dynamics of transcendence can occur.

Rituals in the realm of formal religion serve much the
same purpose as they do in Pernell Andre's life in that they
help persons order their lives. Adult's and children's rituals
inter-connect, for their roots are the same. Both encourage
transcendence in that they permit a leaning beyond the immediate experience. In settings within formal religious traditions, such leanings beyond the known into the unknown are
guided by ritual elders who, within the community of faith,
invoke sacred space—a space laden with expectation, transcendence, and mystery. Often invocation calls for that
which limitlessly transcends and may often be named as
"God."

Both ritual process theory and Lev Vygotsky's (1978)
conceptualization of the zone of proximal development
(from the professional literature of child development and
education) help us better understand the core conditions
introduced in the previous chapter as being necessary for
a spirituality of caring with young children. The chart
below can help us focus more clearly on the resulting conversation.

Dynamics of Movement from the Known to the Unknown

Core Conditions	Vygotsky	Ritual Process Theory
hospitable space	zone of proximal development	invocation of sacred space
recognition of experience	connection to what child can not yet do on his or her own	liminality
adult presence	mentor, coach, teacher, etc. as more knowledgeable other	ritual elder
expectation of transcendence	expectation of transcendence	expectation of transcendence

Hospitable Space, Vygotsky's Zone, and Invocation

Hospitable space can be almost interchangeable with Vygotsky's understanding of a zone of proximal development and with Jennings's understanding of ritual process; yet, each term gives a slightly different perspective to what it is that I am trying to describe. The term "hospitable space" provides us with more of a sense of location while "zone of proximal" suggests an overlapping and permeable edge. If we add to these two concepts the ritual use of invocation, I believe we have begun to identify what occurs in a process of transcendence. Although all of these components (location, edge, and process) are embedded in each of these terms, as suggested above each term can be viewed as having a specific emphasis.

When theologians use the term "invocation," they are clear about the need for an intentional "invoking," a moment which I understand to be significant in any process of transcendence. When we are working with young children we "invoke" by including certain essential "tools/materials" (blocks, easels, sand, clay, picture books, and other such things). Assumptions are made by early-childhood professionals that young children will develop emotionally, socially, physically, and cognitively when they play with such things.

Within the ritual process of a formal religion, sacred space is invoked through the use of familiar objects, gestures, words, and other symbols. The tools of ritual are often every-day things, for example, the tools used within the Christian tradition include bread, wine, water, and candles. Such ritual tools serve the same invoking purpose for religions that a special blanket or toy does for a child at nap time.

It is not by accident that preschool teachers visit in-coming young children in the children's home and provide them with the opportunity to visit the preschool before regular attendance is expected. A familiar object brought by the child into the new space of the preschool sometimes mediates the newness with what is familiar. And if a "new" child discovers things in the "new" place that are similar yet dissimilar from those at home, "invocation" is about connecting the two and giving permission to enter and to feel comfortable with this "new" space.

By the use of such objects, the young child is invited to bring the wholeness of his or her being into the new location, along with all of the ways he or she has learned to make sense of the world in his or her young life. These include the strong feelings of the moment such as anger, joy, jealousy, and anxiety, as well as the skills the child has acquired from experience. No matter what the task or condition, the child in all "childness" is welcome, for the space is hospitable.

Vygotsky's delineation of a zone of proximal development can be envisioned as interlocking circles (adult and new experience/young child and new experience); the overlapping area of the two circles represents the integrating experience of the zone, touching the child on the edge of development.

The overlapping zone suggests that there is something that the child does not yet fully know how to do. Such a perspective takes away value judgements that assign labels such as "bad," "dumb," or "not cooperating" and suggests instead that the child is trying to figure something out. This approach was emphasized by John Dewey as he linked problem-solving to a child's experience within community. There is a problem to be solved. It may be how to behave in a new place, how to relate to new people, or how to use the toilet. The ritual process (including the proper words, gestures, and tools) of invocation incorporates procedures which the culture sees as appropriate for assisting the transcendence of the child in the present state of not yet knowing how they might solve the problem.

Such tools may become more or less mysterious as the child negotiates the zone of proximal development. If they are concrete in nature (such as a potty chair, a spoon, sleeping in a new bed, or getting along with a new baby), the mystery will be gradually understood with the coaching of caring adult presences. If the mystery involves abstractions (such as knowing an ultimate being), the mystery becomes more complex. Such complexity can be manageable (but not fully understood) if adults give a clear message that having such a mystery is meaningful and that it is OK that the young child is not yet able to understand it.

Recognition, Connection, and Liminality

Once the necessity of hospitable space is recognized, organized, and invoked, we can assume this space as the condition of the preschool that surrounds the young child and the life experiences he or she brings into it. If a child throws things about the room (as Pernell Andre did in the earlier days of his development at the Head Start Center), the child is a child who throws things. If the child wants to tie her shoes, she is a child who wants to tie her shoes. If the child is waiting for the arrival of a new baby sister, he is a child who is waiting for the arrival of a new sister. Hospitable space is the space in which old and new experiences are accepted, dealt with, and transcended.

Hospitable space assumes that transcendence from the known to the unknown can occur. The question for any caring adult is: "Given a specific child's past or present experience, what is the next step for this child?" The question that immediately follows can become: "Given what I know about young children and this particular young child, how might I help him or her take that step?" Such a positioning of the new within the experiential background of what is known assumes that some "up in the airness" (liminality) will need to be negotiated.

Hospitable space and the zone of proximal development can be favorably compared with what the psychologist/theologian, Robert Moore (also building on the work of Victor Turner) delineates as "sacred space." Sacred space, like the zone of proximal development and hospitable space, also assumes that transcendence will occur.

Moore (1984) advocates that "sacred space cannot be generated by a simple act of will." Invocation invites the possibility of sacred space. It, too, is a co-creation of two or more persons. There is also a presence of the ultimate that is beyond the immediacy of the moment within such sacred space. Within a Judeo-Christian perspective this presence is called God (the one who limitlessly transcends). Other religious traditions refer to Allah. Black Elk, a holy man of the Sioux, named the ultimate, Wakan-Tanka. With both hospitable space and the zone of proximal development there is the recognition of the existence of more than the immediate relationship, but this "something more" is not always addressed or named. However, some implicit connection is often assumed.

Within religious traditions, Moore uses the term "ritual elders" to name those who help establish sacred space—that space in which students, youth, young children, and all of us enter if we choose to move from the known to the unknown. For Moore, such ritual elders must be adequate stewards of the boundaries of sacred space. To steward such space is to positively deal with boundary issues, assure safety and provide direction and closure. Moore would call such ritual elders "technicians of the sacred" (1984, p. 136).

Within hospitable space those who work with young chldren help them to be with others in a manner that allows everyone to carry on the activities of the moment. Such assistance involves the use of techniques well known to all coaches, mentors, parents, teachers, and more knowledgeable peers. These include figuring out what it is that the child does not yet know how to do; providing models, additional information, and tools as resources to assist in the learning; setting appropriate limits; and, providing constructive feedback. Were we to borrow from Moore, such activity makes us "ritual elders" in our relationships with young childen.

When we engage a child in what Vygotsky terms the zone of proximal development, we are not passive observers, rather, we enter an intersubjective space where, with the child, we co-construct reality. To borrow from Moore again, we are "technicians of the sacred." Using Bruner's word, we provide the "scaffolding" that supports development. Just as Vygotsky described more knowledgeable others within the zone of proximal development, Moore wants ritual elders to be proactively involved in stewarding and invoking sacred space. Both ritual theory and the zone of proximal development assume a common task—that of providing "scaffolding"—as centrally important to facilitating change (be that developmental change in the field of child development, or transformative change in theology). "Scaffolding" is needed because as a change occurs, one steps into the unknown. Writing within a Judeo-Christian tradition, Dow Edgerton (1985) puts it like this:

> The old structure is suspended, the new is not yet in place. The person or group has crossed a boundary—

not unlike the flight out of Egypt—and inhabits a kind
of wilderness. In this wilderness the old structures,
both personal and social, no longer apply. The ordered
meanings beyond the crossed boundary are no help.
Now order is supplied through the presence of powerful symbols, and the ritual elder who understands their
application; now new meanings are shaped and a new
future is prepared. Now the boundary is crossed once
again, but in a different direction. The movement is
into a new situation, not a return to the old. Transformation has occurred. Without the deconstruction of
the old structure and status, change does not occur.
Old wineskins can't hold new wine. (p. 14)

And so Pernell Andre, a boy who threw things, becomes a
child with productive ways of asserting himself.

Presence: A Systems Approach

Because the four core conditions are not watertight com-
partments, much of what needs to be said about presence
can be inferred from the two previous discussion of the core
conditions; nevertheless, be it "ritual elder" or mentor,
coach, teacher, or parent, an authentic adult presence is necessary for a spirituality of caring with young childen. But
what does this look like?

Both at home and in his Head Start Center, Pernell Andre
had others who stood by him and assisted him through
overwhelming and turbulent times. But the presence that he
came to know extended beyond his mother, grandmother,
the Head Start staff and the other children with whom he
played. The relatedness of those who cared for Pernell
Andre went beyond blood and kin ties. The presence of caring adults in Pernell Andre's life was systemic.

The African Methodist Episcopal Church on the north
side of Pittsburgh that housed Pernell Andre Decker's feder-

ally funded Head Start Program was just two doors away from Pernell's home. The pastor was a familiar figure in the Head Start Center and in the community. It was not unusual for him to be seen holding wooden boards while young children pounded nails or enjoying a snack of juice and popcorn while sitting with a group of energetic youngsters.

While the pastor did not use religious language in the Head Start Center, he understood, like the theologian Paul Tillich (1978), that "We can speak to people only if we participate in their concerns; not by condescension, but by sharing . . . " (p. 207). His presence was felt not only by the children but also by the staff.

The pastor felt that the mission of the Head Start Center that was attended by Pernell Andre and his friends was similar to that of the church and the community he served. He worked hard to interpret that belief to his congregation.

Although the Head Start staff was responsible on a day-to day-basis for the arrangement of time and space and paid a nominal fee for electricity, heating, and water, there were others who were a presence for Pernell Andre and his friends in different kinds of ways. These included those who served on the board of trustees of the church and the janitor and other church members who agreed to share and care for their building. Pernell Andre also frequently met friendly faces on the community streets near the church as he was coming and going from the Head Start Center.

Together, the federal government, as an agency of the people of the United States, in partnership with the Pittsburgh Public Schools (funded by the taxpayers of Pittsburgh and Pennsylvania), and the members of the small African Methodist Episcopal Church, provided a place where young children and their families could transcend their present circumstances. Such a partnership involved people on a number of levels who were willing to advocate for young children so that such a partnership might develop. Some of these folks took risks, others shared expertise. Some shared resources including time and money, others cut through red tape. All were willing to cross the borders occasioned by class, race, and circumstance.

Programs such as Head Start require the commitment of all of us, for each one of us has the ability to make meaning within the circumstances in which we live. We can bring together the resources necessary to form a relational partnership and work towards the creation of a spirituality of caring for young children in our communities.

Expectation of Transcendence

The very term "zone of proximal development" as used by Vygotsky suggests that development will occur and that young children will move from the known to the unknown. For many families, the compartmentalization of parent support systems throughout various social institutions (private therapists, hospitals, social service agencies, churches and other institutions) fails to consider the importance of such extended relationships even as they (in isolation from one other) try to support transcendence. This prevents the necessary institutional "border crossings" and confuses young children who are often already stressed by the present circumstances of their lives.

Sometimes adults, too, become overwhelmed and unable to access what they need to help them care for their young children. This becomes more difficult, even toxic, when systems that parents have been able to figure out and make use of break down or become frayed or non-existent. A spirituality of caring requires that we transcend such conditions and become more of a collective, systematic, hospitable presence for all of our young children if they are to engage in transcendence—that movement in their lives from the known to the unknown.

seven

On Spiritualities

The first peace, which is the most important, is that which comes within the souls of men [sic] *when they realize their relationship, their oneness, with the universe and all its Powers, and when they realize that at the center of the universe dwells* Wakan-Tanka *and that this center is really everywhere, it is within each of us.*

—*Black Elk*

No child, no parent/child dyad, no family exists in a vacuum. Child rearing involves community and caring networks of people. Any use of the term spirituality implies that there is something beyond the individual; yet, in today's western culture spirituality is often viewed as individualistic, as a way which individuals can privately draw strength in isolation from "otherness." This conceptualization of a spirituality that exists outside of community is dangerous.

Writing from within the Christian tradition, John Elias (1991) suggests four individualistic interpretations of a reawakened spirituality within the U.S.A. His work provides a frame for further thought about spirituality and young children. While Elias develops this theory from within his own tradition, examining it may be helpful to all of us.

The four individualistic interpretations of the emerging interest in spirituality that Elias suggests are: (1) a spirituality in which the individual is paramount, (2) a spirituality in which human beings are viewed ultimately as "good," (3) a spirituality in which human beings are viewed ultimately as "bad, and (4) a spirituality in which the individual remains primary while community is reduced to an ancillary role. Each of these interpretations is explored below.

Just Me: Excessive Individualism

"Spirituality as the Narcissistic Flight from Social Engagement" (Elias, p. 458), focuses on what Elias understands to be a culture of excessive individualism. In this perspective, individuals work at spiritual growth with considerable intentionality, often through self-help books and support groups. They may assign mystical powers to personal items such as stones, bangles, and other objects. The task is to jump start an inner life and to further develop the spiritual dimension of that life.

Elias suggests that excessive individualism promotes the ignoring of political concerns while resisting engagement with others in order to embrace a world in which self-improvement is paramount. Such a stance often has other-worldly, ascetic, and perhaps austere or celibate overtones. It leads to self-absorption.

Interpersonal relations for someone who believes in such an interpretation of spirituality may be shallow and constructed in order to protect the person from being hurt. It is not the experience of community but self-validation that drives one to enter a group seeking this understanding of spirituality. For Elias, this interpretation may be a necessary (yet unfortunate) response to the bureaucratic nature of modern capitalism in which the self can be easily over-looked or ignored.

The strength of the excessive individualism position is that there is an advocacy for self—a belief that the "I" of autonomous individuals is important. Certainly this is true, yet something is missing here. Elias challenges us to attend to the degree to which such spiritualities "foster a preoccupation with the self at the expense of interpersonal and communal dimensions" (p. 459). I would add that it is difficult to see others, especially young children, when we are self-absorbed. An egocentric interpretation of spirituality does not accept or encourage communal nurture from the extended network in which a child develops.

Such an individualistic, self-centered spirituality may even take the adult out of relationships with young children and those who share in the care and education of the child. It is well documented that many parents and guardians of children simply "opt out" of responsible relationships with them. Issues of spirituality are addressed by such parents through toxic or absent modalities. Some readily relinquish any active role in this area by assuming that as their children grow, they will choose what they want to do for themselves. What is forgotten in such assumptions is that children come to know through active participation in community, and that self-absorption as a value taught to children negates the role of community.

If we use Vygotsky's theory mentioned earlier, we can see young children abandoned when entering a zone of proximal development demarcated more by toxicity than by hospitable space. When self-absorption is supreme, there can be no sacred space (a place of transcendence) as there is little priority given to the "otherness" of self or to other people. An individualistic focus puts children at risk in a variety of ways.

Embracing Naiveness: People Are Good

In a second category, "Spirituality as Self and World Transcendence," Elias includes the self-absorption of the first category, but suggests that here "self-absorption is only a by-product of more encouraging cultural changes" (p. 459). Progress is the key to a recognition of this position. Within this interpretation, exploration and development of self are part of the evolution of a new and improved age.

Self and world transcendence come together as a "spiritual adventure" to reject traditional religions in favor of a personal exploration of more person-centered religions. This is done to prevent the teaching and dogma of traditional religions from getting in the way of religious experience. For this second definition, Elias concludes that "Spirituality is a way of breaking with past forms and speaking about a new world" (p. 462).

While at first glance this second understanding of spirituality may appear to be as self-absorbent and egocentric as was "excessive individualism," advocates of this interpretation argue that it is but "a passing phase in a development of sensibility that will eventually reconcile and transform self, society, humanity, and nature" (p. 460). When it arrives, this new society will value community over competiveness and blend with nature instead of destroying it. While a utopian vision drives this perspective, a personal adventure into spirituality is seen as an important milestone on the way to the new society. Good for all ultimately comes from getting in touch with the "good" self. In this "human beings are innately good" view, once the self develops into a more spiritual being, the world will also become more spiritual. Individual goodness leads, via this spirituality, to a better world.

Elias suggests that this interpretation is also limited since, "Many darker elements of American culture must be ignored to arrive at such an optimistic reading of the contemporary situation" (p. 462). Certainly in relation to the care and education of young children, this second interpretation presents an overly rose-colored world with little room to understand the complexity of one's own feelings and experiences. There is no room for evil, no shadowside of humanity, no child abuse, no negligence. When violence, brutality, rage, fear, and injustice are somehow denied as being part of our human condition, young children grow up unprepared to move past the "safeness" of an isolated world.

Even when the badness outside the "good" world is recognized, the complexity of young children's existence within community is not. Activities such as asking young children to bring toy guns to school to be burned (as suggested by one early-childhood program) are representative of this view of spirituality. This act suggests that a limited understanding of young children is operating. In spite of what young children might understand about toy guns, it is a fantasy to think that if we can somehow eliminate evil—in this case violence in the form of guns—we can become "good" people.

In considering a concept of spirituality that views the nature of humans as "good," I am reminded of an on-going, and educational, experience with my own son and guns. When he was born, I determined that my son was not going to play with guns. There was already too much violence in the world. Fortunately for my son, my husband was not as convinced as I was of this stance, having grown up in Western Pennsylvania where "buck fever" was a legitimate excuse for absence from school during deer hunting season. Nevertheless, we did not provide Jason with play guns.

At the age of two-and-a-half, seated at the breakfast table, our son chewed his toast into a gun and with a huge grin "shot" at the rest of us. By the time he was eight he had an arsenal of handmade guns crafted from sticks, boards, cans, and other "found" materials. He also had a substantial collection of homemade swords, knives, and shields. His play with the neighborhood boys often involved digging foxholes and building forts. (He also however, took part in the plays produced by his sisters and enjoyed sports and music, much to my relief.) When he was ten, he confided to me that while he liked to play with guns, he couldn't really ever shoot anything, even a bird.

I wonder what it would have meant for him to be asked, at the age of three or seven or nine, by well-meaning adults to burn his toy guns. It seems that whenever we take away play things in such an arbitrary fashion we have failed to address the issues that necessitate the play. If people were basically good, it would simply be the task of doing the "good," but people are much more complex. An adequate concept of spirituality must abandon this second definition as too naive.

The Survivalist: People Are Bad

Elias suggests that a third interpretation of spirituality (termed "The Minimal Self in Search for Psychic Survival)" is something of a flip side of the second interpretation. Rather than viewing the world as innately good, it suggests that the world is innately bad. This analysis, according to Elias, "focuses squarely on the psychological effects of the global problems which people perceive as the great problems of the time: war, pollution, terrorism, and industrial failure" (p. 462).

The psychological task for those who hold this view is to develop a new, minimal self that can produce techniques for surviving all of the catastrophes which are viewed as imminent. For Elias this approach sums up a "contemporary interest in spirituality which might be interpreted as an attempt to fashion a self that can survive the impending catastrophes of modern society" (p. 463).

This third interpretation is also preoccupied with the self. It differs in that its focus has now turned to survival rather than growth. Someone outside this position might ask, "How does ones' survival relate to the rest of the world? Can one exist outside of community and commitment? Can one be a whole person while existing in a vacuum?"

Certainly the movie industry has taken this concept to the bank in one-hundred different scenarios. Some of the resulting films are bleak and unremitting in their depiction of the solitary survivalist; still others open the door to the central question: "Can one survive and thrive alone?" This isolationist stance presents a scary view of the world from an egocentric perspective, allowing little discovery for either community or the awe and joy of life. Ultimately it does not offer any sense of hope for our world. One might just as well move to a remote location (for example, Jonestown) where adults self-destruct and destroy children because the "bad" world has gotten too close. And some people do just that, psychically taking their young children with them. They live in isolation, protecting themselves from the evil of others, and at the same time depriving themselves of the joy that can result from being part of a community. As recent tragedies remind us, this third construction of spirituality often is adopted at the risk of young children's lives.

Religion and the Renewal of Commitment and Community

Elias' fourth interpretation of today's spirituality which he terms "Spirituality as the Individual's Renewal of Commitment and Community" (p. 464) is built upon the work of Robert Bellah and his colleagues (1985). Elias criticizes the previous three approaches to spirituality for their failure to "move beyond, integrate, or transform individualism with a spirit of commitment and community" (p. 464).

With Bellah and others, Elias suggests that the uncontrolled individualism at the center of the former three interpretations is "the main weakness in the American character" (p. 464). Elias goes on to say that such an individualistic interpretation of spirituality should be "checked by the two forms of religious organizations, the church and the sect." He adds that while individuals may want to declare their independence from organized religion, "the concept of church and sect remind us that we depend on others, that absolute independence is a false ideal" (p. 465). Thus in his fourth perspective Elias emphasizes that one cannot have spirituality without a social context and that context is organized religion.

Because this fourth perspective gives the individual a social context (within religious institutions), it is more useful in relation to spirituality and young children. Yet when confined to church and sect, isn't it also limiting? Is not the introduction of formal religion as the arbiter of spirituality a somewhat narrow conclusion?

Whenever we place spirituality within the social context of a religious institution, we place young children at risk. Because of this culture's individualistic underpinnings, we can then (falsely) continue to celebrate the existence of an ultimate being inside the doors of our religious organizations, even as young children huddle outside "our" religion in poorly heated houses which burn like piles of kindling wood when space heaters topple. Without a more widely drawn balance of individual and community, we tend to build faulty constructs of spirituality even when we include a locus in formal religion. Young children often suffer abuse and neglect precisely because such religious constructs encourage self-satisfaction.

Perhaps this fourth stance could be expanded to include Paul Tillich's (1978) emphasis on ultimate concern—that source from which we draw strength and which centers our lives. In Tillich's view, a religion represents a cumulative tradition regarding a communal understanding of "ultimate concern." Churches, mosques, temples, and synagogues are places where such cumulative traditions gather to worship out of a precise understanding of ultimate concern. Organizations other than religious institutions may also be centers of value and power that avoid religious labels and may, in fact, be locations for one's "ultimate concern." Nevertheless, any construct of spirituality can be badly skewed when such ultimate concerns (including religious forms) are focused in ways that turn from a wider understanding of relationship toward excessive individualism.

Beyond Self-Absorption: Carl and Interrelatedness

Elias's conceptualizations of our cultural approaches to spirituality are helpful; yet, accepting a normative concept of spirituality that primarily resides in an individualistic understanding is neither universal nor helpful for a small planet. A usable concept of spirituality for these times must be constructed with nurture and care in mind, as well as permeable, interrelated boundaries represented by terms like self, community, world, and cosmos.

Centering on such relatedness, Ross Snyder (1968) wisely wrote that each person:

> ... is really a whole colony of persons, of inner inhabitants, of people met all during a life. Something of these people has entered into this person forever, so that the person sitting next to you is really a community. In that community live still the father and the mother of this person, the boys and girls with whom he [sic] played

most, the people with whom he went to school, the persons with whom he competed. All the live things of this world that came and interacted with this person are still deep within. (p. 40)

Snyder reminds us that our communities are made up of people who lived in other times and places. We meet them and take them into ourselves through the memories of others, through their writings, their films, and their stories.

Carl is a little boy who is very much a part of who I am, of my internal community. He died at the age of 7, long before I was born, and was buried on a hillside in a cemetery in Oil City, Pennsylvania. His sister, my mother, was a young adult when Carl died of complication from typhoid fever.

Often in the summer on lovely sunny days my mother and my brother, Jack, and I walked the six or seven blocks up Hone Avenue to the cemetery. On those days my mother carried a splint basket containing a trowel, water can, and flowering plants from her garden. At the cemetery my mother would pull the weeds from around a small marker of flowers and add those she brought with her to those that were already blooming there.

Jack and I would play in the freshly turned earth, helping my mother pat the rich, dark Pennsylvania dirt around the newest plants. As we grew older we rolled down the hillside and filled the water can at a nearby fountain. On warm days we splashed each other. When we were a little older and learning to read, we wandered further from our mother as she worked, exploring what for us were ancient epithets on tombstones in an old section of the cemetery.

We knew all about Carl's illness, how difficult it was for my grandmother, grandfather, and mother, how he was loved, treasured, and missed. He liked to play ball with my father when my mother and father (just newlyweds at that time) visited the farm where he lived with my grandparents and my mother's little sisters. Together they made balls out of socks just like my dad and older brother did with Jack and me.

In my mind's eye I could see Carl's blond hair and blue eyes—the ones in our photo album at home. I knew that the water had been tested and that his little sisters (my Aunts Alice, Bib, and Inie) also had typhoid. But they lived; they were grown up and had children of their own. They lived, and he died. He was seven.

My mother washed his hair even after the gangrene had set in the side of his mouth. She held him when he could hardly hold up his head and his tongue was swollen all purple and blue.

The words dead and death were part of our conversations, and they didn't frighten my mother although they made her very sad. It was all right to talk about Carl and ask questions. I knew that Jack and I had vaccinations and that we would never get typhoid. Someday we knew my grandmother and grandfather would be buried next to Carl—when they were old, tired, and worn out. Everybody dies someday and that is OK—though it makes the people still alive who love them sad—especially sad when children die. And the grass was green and the sunshine warm and sometimes on the way home we got a Popsicle at Heath's Market.

Death was part of life and Carl was part of me.

Quite often, today, I am asked to talk to groups of adults—usually parents and teachers—about teaching young children about death, and Carl is part of that, too.

Betty Zane also became part of a community that dwells within. My dad told me the story of how in pioneer times she had bravely run through the gun fire at Fort Henry and back again with the much-needed gunpowder sack flung over her shoulder even as the bullets whistled all around her. She was brave, and she was a girl. Later when I could read well, I read Zane Gray's (her grandson's —or maybe it was her great grandson's) version of the story and I knew at my core that girls could do important things.

Even when exaggerated or artfully composed, the stories we tell about what is of ultimate concern are important. A spirituality of caring that includes children will be about the care and nurture and the telling of stories that connect self and others, world and cosmos.

These people and many others do not reside in some dis-embodied community that I as an individual literally inter-act with in some mystical fashion. Yet, I fully understand how some Africans like Kunonga's friend from Kenya (Chapter 3) can talk with and listen to their ancestors, because my ancestors are also a part of the community that is the "I" that I am.

Indwelling Communities

Cultures vary in their conceptualizations of what makes up an individual and what constitutes community. In some cultures, like the U.S.A., decisions often rest more on what's best for the individual than for the community. Autonomy is encouraged, valued, and celebrated. In other cultures (for example China) decisions rest more on what is thought to be best for the entire community. Such assumptions about how the individual is related to the community are often tacit; that is, unexamined, and therefore uncritically accepted by those who are a part of that particular culture. A spirituality of caring that moves beyond such seeming po-larities must assume that individuals and community are not in some final sense, separable entities.

In any fully examined worldview, a spirituality of caring implies that we are part of the indwelling communities of the "I's" of those infants, toddlers, and other young children we love, care for, and teach. We are neither able to exist only for ourselves or to totally subsume who we are to a given community. Such a condition necessitates relatedness.

A spirituality of caring assumes the condition and process of interrelatedness as necessary for a whole approach to young children. This means that a spirituality of caring is political. It has consequences not only for individuals, but also for communities, and for the world. We recognize such consequences in the ways children are stunted or invited into the world. And we are responsible for the political and social decisions that (in a recognition of relationality) mediate the claims of the individual and the community. Ours is a humbling responsibility.

eight

Transformative Possibilities

We can never finish with stories ... we lay them aside for awhile to collect some threads of thought and see what they make.

—*W. Dow Edgerton*

I began this book by suggesting that the individual lives in relationship with community and the larger world. Spirit is a biological condition of being human. At this point in our understanding of human development, that which ignites spirit remains a mystery. We do know that all human beings in every culture have spirit as a life-giving force. And so, humans naturally engage in the process of transcendence, for transcendence is the essence of who we are as humankind. While spirit fuels transcendence, hope, and the ability to learn, nowhere can it be suggested that having spirit automatically results in humans who have these qualities.

As I write these words, Juvenile Court Judge Carol A. Kelly has sentenced two boys who, at the ages of ten and eleven, dropped a five-year-old named Eric out of a fourteenth-floor window to his death because of his refusal to steal candy for them. The upsurge of ever-younger children engaged in similar murderous behavior prompted my state legislature to change the state law—forbidding imprisonment of anyone under the age of thirteen—to allow imprisonment at age ten. It was this changed law that Kelly used to sentence Eric's killers. The reality of young "superpredators" like Eric's killers prompted an editorial in the *Chicago Tribune* which ended with these words about children: "Increasingly, we wonder not whether they can be saved, but whether we can save ourselves from them" (January 31, 1996).

We can imagine the horror of what it must have been like to be a five-year-old held over the edge of a window ledge gripping the hand of someone about to drop you to your death. But the complexity of the life experience of those two children who judged Eric's life to be of less value than candy is more difficult to fathom. Perhaps for these children, life had little meaning. As the transcript from the trial indicates, theirs was not a trustworthy world. And so Eric died and two children who are described as "remorseless" are in prison under a new law occasioned by a rising number of such incidents.

In what sense can we affirm the presence of a caring, hopeful community for these children? Is it possible that they were seen by the adults who lived with them (in their homes, communities, and city) as children who had no value, that could simply be thrown away; and, did these young boys act out of such a socially co-constructed sense of self? What memories of being individuals within a community did these children bring to the building's ledge? I do not know, but since a law is now needed to incarcerate children, our culture will have more occasion to ask such questions. When our children become our enemies, where is hope?

Trustworthiness: The Basis of Faith

As children grow and move away from a trustworthy base, they expect the world to meet their needs appropriately, as they themselves function competently within it. In Erikson's framework this is called basic trust (basic in that it is not always conscious). When children develop such a sense of basic trust, they can hope. Erikson (1964) describes such hope as "The ontogenetic basis of faith . . . nourished by the adult faith which pervades patterns of care" (p. 118).

James Fowler a scholar who bridges theology and human development, has formulated a stage theory for faith development which impacts scholars and practitioners in both the theological and secular worlds. For Fowler, faith is a "generic, a universal feature of human living recognizably similar everywhere despite the variety of forms and contents of religious practice or belief . . . " (1981, p. 14).

Faith, following James Fowler's definition, is a personal construct. A person's faith, given Fowler's framework, is something that could be articulated and acted upon out of a formal religious tradition. Today I saw a "Praise Allah" bumper sticker on the car immediately in front of me at a stop light. Undoubtedly the driver of the car has the Muslim religion as one such center of "value and power" (Fowler, p. 17).

Children's understanding of faith develops over time through concrete experiences with those who hold, support, communicate, and stand with them. As children begin to develop names for things and events around them, they also begin to label the feelings inside of themselves with the help of caring others. These feelings are sorted by the children and provide a basis for an affective bond with important others and with what James Fowler calls "shared centers of value and power."

Fowler proposes that "shared center(s) of value and power" are those ultimate concerns in which "self and others invest trust and loyalty" (p. 17). These centers might include God, money, the Muslim religion, Hollywood, or the Chicago Bulls. Fowler suggests that such nascent images come to order authority and to offer values which precede a child's conscious ability to abstractly sort out the meaning of such centers of value and power.

Faith as a Shared Triadic Concept

Fowler views faith as a "person's or group's way of moving into the force field of life" (1981, p. 4). Much like Tillich, Fowler's definition of faith is connected to a person's ultimate concern, is not necessarily theocentric, and is often unrelated to formal creeds and dogma. For example, Fowler can easily accept that an ultimate concern could be a person's career, and that such a faith position could result in a life that was ordered and sustained (given meaning) through the practices and values of a specific occupation. "Faith," therefore, for Fowler is not necessarily connected with church, temple, or mosque. Faith, therefore, is another shared construct built, according to Fowler, in an interactive, triadic way: (1) *Self* interacts with (2) *others* and with (3) "*shared centers of value and power*" in a dynamic, relational fashion.

Fowler suggests that "all human associations, including the family are dynamic. The members change and their personal and corporate center(s) of value and power must evolve and be renewed. Nonetheless, the triad, with its depiction of the structure of mutual trusts and localities, discloses the essential conventional pattern of faith as relational" (1981, p. 7). Faith, then, is a relational dynamic in which persons may claim many (or one) center(s) of value and power in their lives.

For Fowler, "faith" could be the relationship of self and others and an ultimate concern for something like the educational and nurturing process connected with the institutions and persons committed to young children. A spirituality of caring as a personal and social construct could move someone "into the force field of life" (Fowler, p. 4) and would identify those who are faithful to such a vision. We act out of such centers of value and power. Faith, in this sense, is a shared construct of meaning, both personal and communal.

Faith and a Spirituality of Caring

For the Christian a shared center of value and power is God; in similar fashion, we could say that for the Muslim a shared center of value and power is Allah. If we are to ask how faith (as understood by traditional religions) connects with, impacts, or is a part of a spirituality of caring for young children, we can say that a traditional faith can be open to an incorporaton of a spirituality of caring as a personal center of value and power. A person who engages in such a spirituality could assign it meaning that identifies it as a co-constructed, overarching, connective canopy from within which a person can derive satisfaction. For others, a spirituality of caring may be part of a personal construct that also includes a formal religious tradition, ("Allah be praised.") as the overarching canopy from which all else is ordered. In this example, the Muslim would attempt to incorporate a spirituality of caring within the worldview espoused by the Muslim faith.

The options are many, when a faith tradition (which is, after all, a personal and a social/historical construction) positions itself favorably in relation to something like a spirituality of caring; the faith tradition can be over, under, of, opposed to, or in (but not of) the described spirituality.

Spirituality thus defined is a constructive process. There are many diverse spiritualities available to us. A "spirituality of caring," however, is constructed in ways that favor the thriving of young children. As it deeply connects with spirit and the process of transcendence in a unique way, it offers a variety of entry points into life's underlying dynamic as it relates to self, others, community, world, and cosmos. We can choose to open ourselves to a spirituality of caring as we better understand the role it can play in our life.

When I claim four core conditions as necessary for a community to embody a spirituality of caring in the lives of young children, I am arguing that out of all possible conditions these are the most helpful. While I have discussed four conditions, no linear progression is implied. They all need to be present in overlapping, mutually informing ways. An authentic adult presence must invoke the possibility of transcendence within the lives of young children and adults. An ethos of possibility (transcendence) implies the gathering of certain materials, skills, and interventions that engage young children in participatory knowing—that knowing which is part of the experiences of living that, with trustworthiness, lean toward the unknown.

Intersubjective Dialogue

Because I am aware that spirituality is not a readily accepted word within the discourse of child development literature, throughout this book I have attempted to suggest how developmental theory actually confirms and adds to our understandings of a spirituality of caring even without using the "S" words. Along the way I caution those who have made certain theories of development into religions, suggesting that being open to other ways of doing things may not be wrong, but just different. Such openness is

necessary if we are to engage in the richness multiculturalism provides us when we work with young children.

Rather than trying to make others like ourselves, together we can co-construct hospitable space where each of
us becomes a subject within intersubjective dialogue. In the
process of doing this we must also become involved in in-
trasubjective dialogues within ourselves that allow us to examine closely and creatively the myths that inform our own
living. Jose Solis (1995), an educational scholar who
crosses borders in his own work, concludes:

> While myths persist in reinforcing the formation of our
> identities, ultimately only deconstructing those myths
> will be able to travel in ways that engender a respect
> for and a solidarity with differences and the transfor-
> mative possibilities that present themselves when dif-
> ferences meet and struggle as power is redefined.
> (p. 169)

Such intersubjective dialogue will have a place where differences may not be resolvable but could be understand-
able. As we consider this possibility, we can learn from two
young children. Mary Pat Martin, an early childhood professional who has spent much of her professional life considering issues related to young children and spirituality,
recorded the following observation in the play yard of an
early-childhood program:

> Daniel and Brian are nose to nose. Daniel—four-and-a-
> half years old being the same age as Brian—is several
> inches shorter, so has to look up as they speak or, like
> now, raise voices at each other. Quite an intense dis-
> cussion is going on. The teacher, knowing that each of
> these good friends can stand on his own, watches. She

hears the word "God." She moves a little closer. They are having a debate about who knows the real God. Is it Daniel who knows God from synagogue? Or is it Brian who knows God through the Holy Spirit in his Pentecostal church?

The teacher cannot hear all that is said. The discussion is heated. At some point these two wise children, realizing that there is no resolution and accepting the fact that they disagree, grin at each other and run off to play together (Myers and Martin, 1993, p. 55)

Rather than fighting further, the children get on with their active co-creation of imaginative play. This is not to suggest that their play will become some sort of mystical romp in a meadowland filled with flowers and butterflies. There will be conflicts to be resolved and decisions to be made if their relationship is to grow. But it is through their play that imagination will flourish.

In their play, Daniel and Brian are doing, on a concrete level, that which we adults have the ability to do on a more abstract level. Just as Daniel and Brian experience otherness through their active play in their preschool, you and I can use our imaginations to understand the otherness of those whose experiences are different from our own. Just as playing together helps young children sort out self from world and gradually (with the guidance of caring older children and adults) figure out how to interact with others in life-enhancing ways, we can imagine together ways of living that can help us coexist in similar ways.

If we are to co-construct that which we do not yet know how to do (care for all of our young children), we must imagine what it could be like if we move forward. With our deeply held beliefs we must also bring, in bell hook's words, ". . . an openness of mind and heart that allows us to face reality even as we collectively imagine ways to move beyond boundaries . . . " (p. 207).

People of all faiths can nurture the spirit of our youngest children when spirituality is understood as an inexhaustible web of meaning interrelatedly connecting self, other, world, and cosmos. Within this web of meaning we can work to provide locations that are hospitable spaces where young children can be themselves—sometimes frightened, joyous, tired, grumpy, exuberant, frustrated, confused, angry, jealous, hungry. In our different ways we can be presences touching the experiences of their lives with the firm hope that they (and we) can transcend our present condition.

Stellaluna, a children's book by Janell Cannon (1993), takes us through the feeling-laden experience of a little fruit bat as she spiritedly transcends the unknown:

> In a warm and sultry forest far, far away, there once lived a mother fruit bat and her new baby.
>
> Oh, how Mother Bat loved her soft tiny baby. "I'll name you Stellaluna," she crooned.
>
> Each night, Mother Bat would carry Stellaluna clutched to her breast as she flew out to search for food.

The delightful, clear, yet provocative illustrations show the owl that strikes Mother Bat knocking Stellaluna out of her arms. Her baby wings are not yet ready to fly and she falls downward. A branch catches the small creature, "trembling with cold and fear" she cries out "Mother." One eye peeks out from her folded wing as she clutches a branch. When she can no longer hold on, she drops downward once again:

> Flump! Stellaluna landed headfirst in a soft downy nest.

And so a mother bird and three little birds take her in. Birds and bird foods differ from fruit bats and fruit bat foods. Stellaluna doesn't much like eating the things birds eat like bugs and worms, for she is a fruit bat. But the little fruit bat is all right. She does bird things and the baby birds, much to the dismay of their mother, try fruit bat antics like hanging upside down on the edge of the nest. The clear illustrations are easily understood by young children and adults alike as Stellaluna and the birds explore their capabilities and discover their differences.

And Stellaluna, through some scary times, finds her way home and finds Mother Bat. After coping with the challenges of re-entry into the fruit bat world, Stellaluna has the experience of rescuing the little birds when they try to fly at night, but can't see a thing.

Against a night blue sky, the final illustration shows us the little fruit bat safely hanging upside down from a branch, her wings encasing three little birds standing on the limb immediately below, their wings also protectively enfolding Stellaluna:

> They perched in silence for a long time. "How can we be so different and feel so much alike?. . ."
>
> "And how can we feel so different and be so much alike?. . ."
>
> "I think this is quite a mystery. . . ."

A mystery is something beyond what we can name and understand at any given time. The "mystery" of the story of Stellaluna is the unfolding of a promise for those whose hope is encouraged more by love than by hatred. And although, we are not storybook characters, the mysteries that persist, both inside and outside ourselves, cry out for a spirited and open-minded exploration.

References

Berryman, J. (Summer, 1985) Children's spirituality and religious language. *British Journal of Religious Education*, 7 (3).

Becker, W. (July, 1994) Spiritual struggle in contemporary America. *Theology Today*. 51 (2).

Bellah, R. et al. (1985) *Habits of the Heart.* Berkeley: University of California Press.

Buber, M. (1958) *I and Thou* (Gregor Smith, Trans.). New York: Scribners.

Brown, J. (1989) *Black Elk's Account of the Seven Rites of the Oglala Sioux.* Norman: University of Oklahoma Press.

Bruggemann, W. (1985) The family as world maker, *Journal for Preachers*, 7.

Cannon, J. (1993) *Stellaluna.* New York: Harcourt Brace.

Carter, S. (1994) *The Culture of Disbelief.* New York: Doubleday.

Chatterjee, M. (1989) *The Concept of Spirituality*: New Delhi: R. N. Sachdev.

The Chicago Tribune (January 31, 1996) Grim reality check on Youth crime. Sec. 1, p. 14.

Coles, R. (May, 1982) The faith of children (in an interview by Robert Ellisberg) *Sojourners Magazine*, 15.

Coles, R. (1990) *The Spiritual Life of Children*. New York: Houghton Mifflin.

Cooke, T. (1994) *So Much*. Cambridge, MA: Candlewick Press.

Davydov, V. (1995) The Influence of L. S. Vygotsky on Education, Theory, Research, and Practice (tr. by Stephen T. Kerr). *Educational Researcher*, 24 (3).

Dewey, J. (1934) *A Common Faith*. New Haven: Yale University Press.

Egan, K. (1992) *Imagination in Teaching and Learning*. Chicago: The University of Chicago Press.

Edgerton, D. (1992) *The Passion of Interpretation*. Louisville, Kentucky: Westminster/John Knox Press.

Edgerton, D. (1985) Worship and transformation in human experience. *The Chicago Theological Seminary Register*. 75(3).

Elias, J. (1991) The return of spirituality: Contrasting interpretations. *Religious Education*. 86(3).

Erikson, E. (1963) *Childhood and Society*. New York: W. W. Norton.

Erikson, E. (1964) *Insight and Responsibility: Lectures on the Ethical Implications of Psychoanalytic Insight*. New York: W. W. Norton.

Erikson, E. (1985) *The Life Cycle Completed*. New York: W. W. Norton.

Erikson, E. As quoted by Bob Green in *The Chicago Tribune* Heiple's Justice and who feels the pain (February 18, 1996) Sec.1, p. 2.

Eyer, D. (1992) *Mother-Infant Bonding: A Scientific Fiction.* New Haven: Yale University Press.

Fowler, J. (1981) *Stages of Faith: The Psychology of Human Development and the Quest for Meaning.* New York: Harper and Row.

Gardner, H. (1993) *Frames of Mind.* Tenth anniversary edition. New York: Basic Books.

Giroux, H. (1992) *Border Crossings.* New York: Routledge

Goggin, H. (1994) The Relationship Between the New Physics and Present Day Images of God. Paper presented at the meeting of the Association of Professors of Religious Education, Chicago, Illinois.

Harris, M. (1989) *Dance of the Spirit: The Seven Steps of Women's Spirituality.* New York: Bantam Books.

Heschel, A. (1991) *No Religion is an Island.* H. Kasimow and B. Sherwin, eds. Maryknoll, NY: Orbis Books.

hooks, bell (1994) *Teaching to Transgress: Education as the New Practice of Freedom.* New York: Routledge.

Huebner, D. (1995) Education and Spirituality *JCT* 11 (2).

Jennings, T. (1995) Making Sense of God. In *Companion Encyclopedia of Theology*, P. Byrne and L. Houlden, eds. New York: Routledge.

Jennings, T. (1982) On Ritual Knowledge. *The Journal of Religious Education,* 62 (2).

Kantrowitz, B. (November 28, 1994) In Search of the Sacred. In *Newsweek.*

Kelly, G. (1955) *The Psychology of Personal Constructs.* New York: W. W. Norton.

Kohut, H. (1985) *Self Psychology and the Humanities: Reflections on a New Psychoanalytic Approach.* New York: W.W. Norton & Company.

Kunonga, N. (1992) The African Principle of Existence-in-Relation as a Model for Cross-Cultural Ministry. In *Knowledge, Attitude and Experience.* Ed. Young-Il Kim.

Nashville: Abingdon Press.

Lonergan; B. (1972) *Methods in Theology*. New York: Herder and Herder.

Merleau-Ponty, M. (1962) *Phenomenology of Perception*. London: Routledge & Kegan Paul.

Moore, R. (1985) Ministry, sacred space, and theological education: The legacy of Victor Turner, *The Chicaco Theological Seminary Register*, 75 (3).

Moore, R. (1984) Space and transformation in human experience. In *Anthropology and the Study of Religion*. Eds. B. Moore and F. Reynolds. Chicago: Center for the Scientific Study of Religion.

Myers, B. and Martin, M. P. (January 1993) Faith foundations for all of our children, *Young Children*, 48 (2).

Myers, B. And Myers, W. (1992) *Engaging in Transcendence: The Church's Ministry and Covenant with Young Children*. Cleveland: The Pilgrim Press.

Noddings, N. (1984) *Caring: A Feminine Approach to Ethics and Moral Education*. Berkeley: University of California Press.

Norris, K. (1993) *Dakota: A Spiritual Geography*. New York: Houghton Mifflin.

Nouwen, H. (1975) *Reaching Out: The Three Movements of the Spiritual Life*. Garden City, New York: Doubleday.

Phenix, P. (1964) *Realms of Meaning*. New York: McGraw Hill.

Phenix, P. (1974) Transcendence in the curriculum. In *Conflicting Conception of Curriculum*, Eds. Elliot W. Eisner and Elizabeth Vallance. Berkeley: McCutchan.

Ryan, A. (1995) *John Dewey and the High Tide of American Liberalism*. New York: W .W. Norton.

Schorr, L. And Schorr, D. (1988) *Within our Reach: Breaking the Cycle of Disadvantage*. New York: Doubleday.

Sloan, D. (Winter, 1989) Educating for a public vision, *The Chicago Theological Seminary Register, 74 (1).*

Snyder, R. (1968) *Inscape.* Nashville: Abingdon Press.

Suchocki, M. (1994) *The Fall to Violence.* New York: Continuum.

Solis, J. (1995) Entre la Marquesina. In *Beyond Comfort Zones in Multiculturalism: Confronting the Politics of Privilege.* S. Jackson and J. Solis, eds. Westport, CT: Bergin and Garvey.

Tillich, P. (1978) *Theology of Culture.* New York: Oxford University Press.

Turner, F. (April, 1995) The Freedoms of the Past: On the Advantage of Looking Backward. *Harper's Magazine.* 290, (1739).

Vygotsky, L. (1978) *Mind and Society.* Boston: Harvard University Press.

Watterson, W. (December 31, 1995) *The Chicago Tribune.*

Wilber, K. (1984) *A Sociable God: Toward a New Understanding of Religion.* London: New Science Library.

Wolff-Salin, M. (1986) *No other light: Points of convergence in psychology.* New York: Crossroads.

Index